WORLD MYTHOLOGY

IN BITE-SIZED CHUNKS

MARK DANIELS

Michael O'Mara Books Limited

This paperback edition first published in 2016

First published in hardback under the title *The Midas Touch* in Great Britain in 2013 by
Michael O'Mara Books Limited
9 Lion Yard
Tremadoc Road
London SW4 7NQ

A CIP catalogue record for this book is available from the British Library.

Papers used by Michael O'Mara Books Limited are natural, recyclable products made from wood grown in sustainable forests. The manufacturing processes conform to the environmental regulations of the country of origin.

ISBN: 978-1-78243-575-4 in paperback print format
ISBN: 978-1-78243-079-7 in EPub format
ISBN: 978-1-78243-080-3 in Mobipocket format

3 4 5 6 7 8 9 10

Designed and typeset by www.glensaville.com
Cover design by Ana Bjezancevic
Cover illustrations © www.shutterstock.com (Dn Br, Hung Chung Chih, Igor Kisselev, Iluistrator, John Lock, Kristina Birukova, LanaN, Maximilian Laschon, Sahua D, Tan Tan, Voropaev Vasiliy, Vector Draco, Zizar)

Illustrations by Siaron Hughes

Printed and bound by CPI Group (UK) Ltd, Croydon, CR0 4YY

www.mombooks.com

WORLD MYTHOLOGY

IN BITE-SIZED CHUNKS

CONTENTS

ACKNOWLEDGEMENTS

My sincerest thanks to all at Michael O'Mara Books, especially to my editor Katie Duce, to Glen Saville for his typesetting and to Siaron Hughes for her illustrations.

INTRODUCTION

Throughout human existence, we have pondered the fundamental questions of life, death, nature and our relationships with one another. Astonishingly, across the globe and across an inordinately long time span, our solutions to these queries have been identical: the creation of myths.

From vast civilizations to localized societies the world over, each has created a rich catalogue of its own deities, monsters and myths. These tell the stories of our origins, triumphs and disasters, and act as creative tools to communicate life's most important lessons.

The majority of religions and mythologies contain key features that point to some of the very basic questions we have been asking ourselves since our early development as a civilized species: concerns around mortality, birth, astrology and nature as a whole. Often we have looked to nature to inspire stories to explain the inexplicable, creating deities from the sun, the moon, rivers, the sea and mountains. In trying to make sense of the unanswerable, we humans have a tendency to subordinate ourselves to a higher power far beyond our comprehension.

Most theologies try to appease these gods and heroes of our own creation through sacrifice, music, dance, prayer and ceremony. Through this we give ourselves a way to comprehend and gain control over hugely important – yet unpredictable – matters such as health and death, the annual harvest or the swell of the sea. These rituals give each society a set of traditions that helps to forge a community identity and an individual notion of belonging.

Cognitive scientists have likened the divine experience we derive from group recitation of prayer to the swell of emotion felt at a huge sporting event. We thrive on the sense of togetherness and social cohesion that we feel from communal ceremony, the joint chorus of prayer, or the unifying chant of a football stadium – and myths give us reasons to create such shared rituals.

And if we don't have stories, legends and religion upon which to base our rituals, what are we left with? The atheist's life is punctuated by weddings, funerals and naming ceremonies that lack the sense of occasion created by the smells, bells and mumbo jumbo of an ancient religious ceremony steeped in tradition, and thick with allegorical lessons and stories as large and old as the universe.

Moreover, the richly imaginative stories of myths and legends serve to make the message within them all the more appealing. A mother telling a child to be nice to other children because it's nice to be nice is not likely to elicit much behavioural change. But if the same message is wrapped up in an ancient story, it – illogically – becomes something much more tangible that a child (or adult, for that matter) can relate to: if you aren't nice to other children, the Greek god Zeus, a big bearded man who lives on a mountain and who carries a lightning bolt, will be most disgruntled. A recitation of some thirty examples of the terrible horrors Zeus has inflicted on other naughty children later and even the storyteller has forgotten that all of this was meant to be allegorical.

World Mythology in Bite-sized Chunks investigates a rich and staggering collection of tales created to help explain the world, taking a roughly chronological peek into some of the most famous and most intriguing stories behind the planet's greatest civilizations. And by the time we're done, you'll be something of a legend yourself.

CHAPTER I:

AUSTRALIAN AND MAORI MYTHOLOGY

Aboriginal Australian Mythology

Although colonized by the British just 225 years ago, Australia's indigenous civilization dates back approximately 70,000 years, and the myths within that culture some 10,000 years. Many of the stories were rooted in the geological features that lay nearby to the tribes that told them. Although the myths were not committed to writing during that period, specific local phenomena described in some stories place those myths within that time frame. It is nothing short of a miracle that the same tales have been passed down from generation to generation, and it is purely by word of mouth the stories survive to be told today.

A colossal landmass, indigenous Australia contained an extraordinary array of roughly 400 distinct tribes, with their own unique language and belief systems. As such, cataloguing just one mythology will barely scratch the surface, so we will instead dip into some of the most fascinating stories from across the whole continent.

Dreamtime

Aboriginal Australian mythology references three main realms – human, land and the sacred realm. During the creation of the world, before human life came into being, there existed an era known as Dreamtime. Following creation, Australian Aboriginals believed people lived simultaneously in both the physical world and in Dreamtime, suggesting that in life and in death an element of each of us resides in the eternal Dreamtime. To better understand and influence the current environment, tribes would sing and pray to the Dreamtime incarnation of whichever person, animal, object or other for which they needed help understanding; for example, appealing to the Dreamtime crocodile to help in controlling the real-life version of the same animal.

The legends of Dreamtime are used as aetiological myths and moral lessons, transposing their lessons onto the lives of their storytellers, and, as such, they remain an important part of Aboriginal culture. Covering such a vast expanse of land, it is understandable that the Dreamtime myths vary from one tribe to the next, and so an individual set of myths becomes very much a part of each clan's identity.

Walkabout

The Aboriginal Australians were – and still are – inextricably linked to the land around them. A hugely important part of their civilization is the concept of 'walkabout', a journey undertaken by adolescent boys during which they retrace the ancient pathways of their ancestors. Along the way, these boys stop at preordained sites and perform a series of traditional ceremonies.

The song and ceremony associated with these journeys of seclusion gave rise to the term 'songlines' to describe the pathways the boys walk upon. These routes criss-cross Australia and link sites such as watering holes, caves, landmarks and notable food sources that are of great importance to different tribes. The young man spends up to several months connecting with the land and with his ancestors through their shared ancient ritual; he learns how to live from the earth itself and to reach contentment and peace through solitude.

He returns, one hopes, a man.

The Rainbow Serpent

Despite the staggering array of belief systems across Australia, one character makes more than one appearance: the Rainbow Serpent. The stories – and names – attributed to her vary, but she is generally associated with water, and therefore life itself. In many stories, she ends up devouring people but also bringing traditions and customs to the people of Australia. The Rainbow Serpent is used as a creation story, as well as an explanation for laws, customs and the totemic tribal culture across Australia.

During Dreamtime, at the very dawn of time, as the serpent travelled across the length and breadth of Australia, the markings of her wandering created the valleys, rivers and creeks. Eventually, she called forward the frogs, which emerged from the earth with heavy bellies full of water. The Rainbow Serpent tickled their stomachs and the water poured out across the world, filling the rivers and lakes. From this all other life – both plant and animal – emerged. The kangaroo, emu, snake, birds and other animals then followed the Rainbow Serpent as she moved across the land, with each animal helping to retain the ecological balance by hunting only for its own kind.

The serpent brought in laws and decreed that those who disobeyed them were to remain in their animal form, while those who were well behaved were upgraded to human form. Each tribe was given a totem of the animal from which they came as their identifying icon and to remind them of their origins. They were permitted to eat everything except their ancestral animal, which meant there would be enough food for everyone – a useful tenet in a land where resources are so scarce.

The Sun

In the very early days of Dreamtime, before the sun was created, a young girl, desperately in love, was forbidden from being with her chosen beau. In frustration, she ran away, fleeing deep into the bush, far from food and protection and encountering increasingly harsh conditions. Her tribe in pursuit, the love-struck girl was forced to enter even more inhospitable places.

Upon seeing the young girl asleep and very close to death, the spirits of her ancestors decided it was time to intervene. They lifted her up into the sky, where she woke to find food to eat and fire to keep her warm. She could see that her people were cold and in the dark, and unable to keep their fires going all day long. So even though she missed her family and longed to return to them, she knew she now belonged to the sky and that it was her duty to help her family.

Building her fire as big as she could, the young girl kept it burning all day long so that her people would have warmth. The creation of the sun brought her much happiness, and she resolved to relight it every day to enable her family to go about their business.

The Moon

One fateful day, a great hunter of the Dreamtime era known as Japara left his wife and young son to hunt down his daily catch. In his absence, Parukapoli, a wandering storyteller, happened upon Japara's wife and sat regaling her with wonderful tales in which she found herself completely lost. Her concentration was broken only by the sudden splashing sound of her son crawling into the stream. She rushed over to save him, but it was too late – the young boy had drowned.

Cradling his lifeless body in her arms, she sat there sobbing all day long waiting for Japara's return. When she explained to him what had happened, her husband flew into a rage and blamed her for the death. He took out his weapons and killed his wife, and then he turned on Parukapoli. The two men fought, both sustaining many injuries, but it was Japara who eventually emerged victorious, killing the storyteller.

Berated by his tribe, Japara soon saw the error of his ways. He went in search of the bodies of his wife and son, but soon found they had disappeared. He lamented his actions and pleaded with the spirits that had taken them away that he be reunited with his family. The spirits acquiesced and allowed Japara entrance into the sky world so he could look for his family, adding that, as punishment, he must search the lonely sky for them himself.

It is said that you can still see the scars from Japara's fight with Parukapoli in the lines on the moon, which is itself a reflection of the campfire he lit to help him in his desperate quest to be reunited with his family. The changing route and shape of the moon is an illustration of poor Japara's endless search.

MAORI MYTHOLOGY

The first Maori settlers arrived in New Zealand (or Aotearoa, as it was known) from Polynesia in the thirteenth century AD. The Maori tradition of New Zealand is entirely independent of Aboriginal Australia, and has been grouped within this chapter for reasons of geography.

Maori tradition has a rich, polytheistic heritage and its myths are deeply entwined with nature. The early Maori people descended from the same Polynesian, Micronesian and Melanesian settlers who had travelled the length and breadth of the Pacific to inhabit islands as far-flung as Hawaii and Fiji. This ancient itinerant history has rendered Maori people in respectful awe of the sea, and may explain why many of their myths contain themes of travel, loss and separation.

Ranginui and Papatuanuku (Sky Father and Earth Mother)

According to Maori mythology, Ranginui (abbrev. Rangi), the Sky Father, and Papatuanuku (abbrev. Papa), the Earth Mother, were the progenitors of all earthly things. In the beginning, there was nothing (a theme common to almost all creation myths), and, within this darkness, Rangi and Papa lay embracing one another tightly for millions of years. The fruits of their bond was a brood of all-male children, all of whom were forced to live in the cramped space between their parents with nothing but blackness surrounding them.

As the young men grew bigger, they became increasingly irate at their predicament and began to argue about how they should separate their parents. Tumatauenga, the god of war and the most belligerent of the brothers, wanted to kill both parents, but luckily it was the plan of Tane-mahuta, god of the forest, the brothers opted for: they would prise their parents apart.

Each child tried in vain to separate Rangi and Papa, but to no avail. The onus was once again on Tane-mahuta, who used his enormous strength to pull the earth away from the sky, bringing light and the first dawn into the world. Devastated at this separation, Rangi rained down tears of anguish, which created the rivers and lakes. Each brother found a role as a result of their parents' split: Tawhirimatea, the god of wind, who had wanted to leave things just as they were, found solace in the sky, later beating down all of brother Tane-mahuta's trees with his gusty power; Tangaroa, the god of the sea, fled Tawhirimatea's fury and found protection in the ocean.

Even today, the grief of the couple's separation can be felt: Rangi continues to cry sad tears, which fall to the earth as rain, and his estranged wife Papa unleashes earthquakes in a vain attempt to break up the land, and therefore the distance, that sits between them. But the two remain separated for ever.

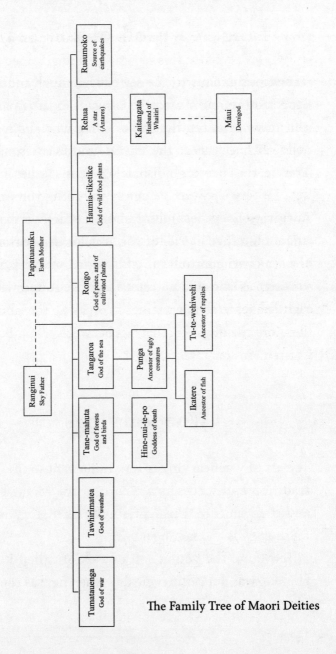

The Family Tree of Maori Deities

Tangaroa (God of the Sea)

Tangaroa's exodus to the sea caused much confusion, especially among his family. Punga, Tangaroa's son and the ancestor of reptiles, sharks, lizards and stingrays, followed his father to the sea. Of Punga's two sons, only Ikatere, the ancestor of fish, followed his father into the sea. Tu-te-wehiwehi, Punga's remaining son and the ancestor of reptiles, found himself stuck on dry land and took refuge in the forests. It is for this reason that the sea continues to be at odds with Tane-mahuta and erodes the land in an attempt to be reunited with his rightful descendants.

Woodcarvings

The art of woodcarving is very important to the Maori tradition and serves as a record of the Maori people and their culture. Unsurprisingly, its history within mythology is an exciting affair.

Te Manu, the young son of a chief called Rua-te-pupuke, was out sailing one day when he was captured by Tangaroa. In desperation, Rua went in search of his son. On finding Tangaroa's home, Rua found it covered in intricate woodcarvings, among which he saw his son dangling from the roof, much like a wall hanging. In a fit of rage, Rua was determined to kill Tangaroa, but was advised by Hine-matikotai, an elderly caretaker, to enter the home and fill up all the cracks and crevices to block out any external light. On entering the home, Rua found it bursting with more woodcarvings, all of which, unlike the carvings on the exterior of the house, appeared to be speaking to each other. Rua addressed them and they agreed to carry out his plan.

Written in Ink

The distinctive, intricate designs of Maori woodcarvings are replicated today the world over in 'tribal' tattoos.

The following morning, all was silent. Tangaroa, his son, grandson and all the other fish tried in vain to wake themselves, but were coaxed back to sleep by the darkness. The scene was set for Rua to take his revenge. Standing outside Tangaroa's silent house, Rua set it on fire. Escapees emerged immediately from the burning building, including Kanae (mullet) and Maroro (flying fish), but with many more fish perishing inside. Rua, too, managed to flee the wreckage, picking up a handful of the exterior woodcarvings en route, bringing the non-speaking version of the art form into the human world.

The intricate patterns seen inscribed in wood are said to be inspired by the patterns of fish scales, which could explain why Tangaroa is associated with them. In honour of the killing of Rua's son, it is traditional for Maori homes to have a gargoyle-style boy (known as a tekoteko) on the rooftop of a house as a protection against intruders.

Tumatauenga (God of War)

Tumatauenga was the most belligerent of Rangi and Papa's offspring. He had wanted to kill his parents in order to separate them and let light into the world. Although his brother Tane-mahuta's more sensible plan was accepted, Tumatauenga's fighting talk did not stop there.

Opposed to the actions of his brothers, Tumatauenga created traps to catch the birds (the children of his brother Tane-mahuta), nets to catch the fish (the children of his brother Tangaroa), and created tools to harvest the land – the fruits of his brother Rongo, the god of agriculture. It is for these reasons that Maoris can happily eat animals, fish and vegetation, even if they are the offspring of the gods. The only one of his brothers Tumatauenga could not tame was Tawhirimatea, the god of wind, who continues to this day to express his foul moods through the medium of bad weather.

Tumatauenga is a crucial deity of enormous stature because he has enabled humans to make full use of the land and sea by eating fish and cultivating crops.

Maui-Tikitiki (Demigod)

Several generations down from Rangi, Papa and their characterful offspring was a demigod known as Maui, responsible for many exploits. As a young boy, Maui would watch jealously as his older brothers went out fishing in their canoe and returned with a haul of fish. He would beg every day to be allowed to go with them, but they refused, mocking his youth and size. Not to be deterred, Maui sat down in secret and, using a traditional Maori incantation (a karakia), prayed for his fishing line to be given extra strength.

Maui hid himself in the fishing canoe and his brothers set out to sea. When they were far out, Maui revealed himself – much to the dismay of his siblings – and promised they would catch more fish than ever with him there. As his brothers swung their lines, Maui sang out his karakia and very soon the little canoe was filled with fish. Next, it was Maui's turn. Using his own blood as bait on the hook made from the magical jawbone of his grandmother and chanting his invocations, Maui cast his line, which travelled far down into the world of Tangaroa. When it became taut, it was clear Maui had happened upon a significant catch. Their canoe was dragged from side to side and pulled along by the mighty fish, forcing Maui's brothers to beg him to cut the line. But he held tight and eventually reeled in what can only be described as a *really* big fish.

While his brothers guarded the fish, Maui went back to his people in Hawaiki (the mythical homeland of the Maori people, and from the same linguistic root as the word Hawaii) to get their help in bringing the big fish home. But on their arrival back at the canoe, Maui and his helpers found the greedy brothers hacking away at the fish, claiming parts of it for themselves. Luckily, however, the fish was so enormous that all the people and animals of Hawaiki were able to fit on it. The big fish became the North Island of Aotearoa (New Zealand), and the mountains and valleys are evidence still of the brothers' greedy hacking. Maui's canoe was also inhabited as the country's South Island. Even today, the Maori names for the islands of New Zealand are Te Ika-a-Maui ('the fish of Maui') for the North Island and Te Waka-a-Maui ('the canoe of Maui') for the South Island.

Hine-Nui-Te-Po
(Goddess of Death)

Hine-nui-te-po was the daughter of Tane-mahuta (god of the forest), but he also took her as his wife. When she discovered that he was in fact her father, Hine-nui-te-po fled to the underworld in shame, whereupon she became its ruler.

Despite the many achievements of Maui, which included slowing the course of the sun so that light lasted all day, he lived in the knowledge that he would one day die, following an omen cast over him by his father on the day of his baptism. Not to be cowed by such trivialities, Maui resolved to visit Hine-nui-te-po and trick her into granting him immortality.

Ahead of his visit, Maui gathered together a flock of different birds to take as his companions. He then made his way to the goddess, who could be seen as the red glow on the western horizon. A startling physical presence, Hine-nui-te-po's hair resembled seaweed, her mouth a barracuda, and she had eyes of bright-red stone. When Maui and his companions reached her, she was asleep on her back with her legs wide open, in between which they could see sharp shards of volcanic glass and rock.

This was the entrance to the underworld.

Maui gallantly removed his clothes, revealing the intricate fish-scale patterns of his Maori tattoos, and entered in between Hine-nui-te-po's legs with his entire body. Although he had begged his avian friends not to make a stir until they saw him emerge from the goddess's mouth, the absurd scene was too much for one little bird, who let out an excited chirrup of laughter.

Hine-tui-te-po awoke immediately and crushed Maui in two with her razor-sharp vagina and he became the first living thing to die. It is because of Maui's experience that all Maori people must experience death.

CHAPTER 2:

SUMERIAN MYTHOLOGY

WHO WERE THE SUMERIANS?

Ancient Mesopotamia shown against present-day borders

The Sumerians were an ancient civilization that lived in Sumer, in southern Mesopotamia, from *c.* 4000 BC. The name 'Mesopotamia' was coined by the Greeks and it referred to the land 'between the rivers' Euphrates and Tigris, in what today is Iraq and Syria. In fact, it was the flash flooding of these rivers that some Christians regard

WORLD MYTHOLOGY IN BITE-SIZED CHUNKS

as the inspiration for the Biblical story of Noah and his ark, and Sumerian mythology itself also contains tales of a destructive flood. Interestingly, geologists have found evidence of several very serious floods in the region from 4000 BC to 2000 BC. Although, it seems that flood myths together with the idea of destruction and cultural rebirth are common: we see similar tales told by the Greeks, the Romans and the indigenous Central Americans (see more on Mayan floods on page 111). And it is of course likely that evidence of floods can be found near most confluences of large rivers.

People settled in the region from the fifth century BC, and communities that were later to become large city-states were founded. Over the following millennium, Semitic people known as the Sumerians migrated in from all sides, including from the Syrian and Arabian deserts, and the region began to flourish. Their glory days lasted until about 2300 BC, making them one of earth's earliest civilizations. However, eventual infighting between the city-states weakened their united power against outside forces (a common error that has seen the downfall of many civilizations, including the Roman Empire). The Sumerians were the proud creators of one of the earliest forms of writing, a syllabic alphabet now known as cuneiform, and their knowledge in early astronomy and mythology alike went on to influence many other civilizations, including the Greeks.

In the Very Beginning

The fragments we have of Sumerian text are just that – and so piecing together their stories is tricky at best. Their cuneiform alphabet wasn't deciphered until the nineteenth century, but their texts tell us of the kings (some real, some mythical), gods and cosmology of this ancient civilization.

In one fragment, we can see a start to the creation of the universe that is common to several other belief systems: the separation of the earth and the sky. In the case of the Sumerians, it is the sky god, An, and his female counterpart of the earth, Ki, who are separated by their son, Enlil. He later overthrows his father to become the king of the pantheon of gods.

In another fragment of text, the goddess of the air, Ninlil, is warned against bathing naked in the river, should it attract the unwanted attentions of Enlil. Inevitably, Ninlil blithely finds her way down to the river at the first opportunity, where she is accosted by the enamoured Enlil and impregnated with the moon god Nanna. Appalled by this behaviour, the other deities banish Enlil from the land of the gods, sending him and his pregnant lover towards the underworld.

Enlil seemingly can't bear the thought of his son being consigned to such an eternity, and so devises a plan that, to modern-day audiences, may seem a touch illogical: he disguises himself as three different characters in the underworld – a gatekeeper, the river owner and the ferryman – each of whom impregnates the poor Ninlil. When she gives birth to her various offspring, including the three lesser deities, Nanna is free to ascend to the sky where he belongs, leaving his parents and siblings behind.

A Modern Myth From the Sumerians

The tablet shown here was created from a cylindrical carved stone, which was then rolled over clay to imprint an image. These cylinder seals were used as official stamps and even worn as jewellery by Sumerian dandies, with each cylinder depicting a different scene. The one below pictures a leader of some sort officiating at a ceremony between two people, and it has caught the imagination of many modern-day conspiracy theorists because of the alleged appearance of the sun and planets in the sky.

The Sumerian cylinder seal imprint that implies ancient knowledge of our solar system

In between the two standing characters can be seen what looks to be the sun surrounded by eleven celestial bodies, with a twelfth one further away towards the seated character. Zecharia Sitchin published a book in the 1970s about the significance of this imprint, claiming that the eleven dots resembled the nine planets of our solar system, alongside two of its moons – thus making this an extraordinary example of the Sumerians' knowledge of astronomy and their understanding of the solar system many thousands of years ahead of anyone else.

But he didn't stop there. According to Sitchin, the mysterious twelfth dot outside of the 'solar system' represents a planet called Nibiru, from which aliens would come to visit the Sumerians every 3,600 years to experiment on them, teach them things and fornicate with their wives. He states that the myths that tell of the Anunnaki gods coming to the mortal world were in fact these alien excursions and not (as most would believe) just the visits of gods descended from An.

There are a few problems with this theory – most crucially that, in surviving texts, the Sumerians describe their worldview, which is akin to the idea held by other early civilizations that the earth is flat, with a deathly underworld beneath it, all surrounded by celestial water. No mention is made of the sun and the solar system. Nonetheless, this theory has captivated some people's minds, and the Internet is awash with theories of aliens from 'Planet X' visiting the earth every few millennia, despite the fact that no one thought to record such a visit in the intervening excursion that must have occurred between the Sumerians' heyday and today.

However, this goes to show our general willingness to latch on to myths and believe any story to rationalize the inexplicable. Conspiracy theorizing is just another example of myth-making – a non-religious approach to creating a higher being that holds the secrets to the world's mysteries.

GODS AND HEROES

The Sumerians created an extensive pantheon of gods. There are many characters in their myths that are cognate with deities in other mythologies – such as gods dedicated to the sky, the earth, the sea, the moon and war.

The fragments of Sumerian texts that we have deciphered tell us of their early founding gods, and depict them as the first kings of their great city-states, from whom their governing families were descended. This helped set their kings on the highest pedestal possible, and was an excellent way to exalt the leaders to the status of semi-divine – after all, who would dare defy one of the gods' great-great-great-grandsons? This tool was also employed by the Romans – see how Augustus used the story of Aeneas to his benefit on page 174.

Enki

The gods inhabited the idyllic land of Dilmun, where all creatures lived in harmony. Nintu, a female deity, asked Enki, one of the most important Sumerian gods, to produce rains. As the god of water, Enki obliged and, possessing a voracious sexual appetite, tried also to woo Nintu. Giving divine significance to marriage, the Sumerian tale states that Nintu did not indulge Enki's passions until he had made an honest woman of her.

Unfortunately, that is where the honesty ended. Nintu was pregnant for nine days before she gave birth to Ninsar (goddess of plants), who was in turn impregnated by her father. Following a mere nine days of pregnancy, Ninsar gave birth to Ninkurra, the goddess of mountains. Not to break with tradition, Enki impregnated Ninkurra, who in turn gave birth to Uttu. He was also able to woo Uttu into sleeping with him, making her the fourth generation to do so.

At the end of her tether, Nintu removed the latest 'seed' from Uttu's body and planted it in the ground, from which grew eight plants. Not content with having caused enough mischief, Enki decided the plants looked delicious and promptly ate them. But, lacking the necessary body parts to give birth to these offspring,

Enki became sick and experienced swelling in eight places around his body.

Nintu eventually came to his rescue, extracting his semen and giving birth to the eight goddesses herself. Each of these goddesses is associated with the healing of the eight different body parts that were affected in Enki: the mouth, the jaw, the ribs, and so on. The myth acts as an important lesson in the follies of excess, as well as explaining the growth of life (both plant and human) and providing deities to pray to for a variety of ailments.

Gilgamesh and the Flood

The story of Gilgamesh is possibly the oldest story ever to have been written down, so it certainly deserves retelling. Gilgamesh was a king of the ancient city of Uruk in *c.* 2500 BC, and, from the many different fragments of tablets that tell of his story, we have been able to piece together the legends that surround him. He was said to be a mortal descended from the gods – rich, powerful, beautiful and absurdly strong, but with that came greed, arrogance and a voracious sexual appetite.

The gods sent him an adversary in the form of Enkidu to fight him while he was engaged in a sexual assault – but the plan backfired as the two eventually became firm friends. Finally, Gilgamesh had found a partner in crime who was also a demigod, and just as willing to cause havoc. The gods had to intervene once more when the two overstepped the mark by felling some sacred trees and slaying a cherished bull sent by Ishtar (goddess of love) who had been jilted by the handsome Gilgamesh. The gods decreed that Endiku should be afflicted by a ghastly disease that would lead to death, leaving Gilgamesh to reflect on the possibility of his own death. He then set out on a mission to find out the secret to gaining immortality.

Following all manner of adventures too numerous to detail, Gilgamesh eventually encountered Utnapishtim – a man who had been granted immortality by the gods – and listened avidly to his story. Utnapishtim told how the council of gods had decided that, having tired of the human race, they would command a great flood to kill everyone and start all over again. Only Utnapishtim was told of the imminent flood in a dream by Ea, the god of wisdom, who instructed him to build a huge wooden boat to carry his family and all the animals and plants to safety. When the flood arrived, everyone but Utnapishtim and his menagerie of animals was washed away. After a few weeks at sea, Utnapishtim let loose three birds, the last of which finally signalled to his master that there was land nearby and they had therefore reached safety.

Enthralled by this story, Gilgamesh contented himself with the knowledge that his individual mortality was bearable since that of mankind as a whole was immortal. He returned to Uruk mortal, but certainly happier, and satisfied that his legacy would live on for ever – as has been borne out by the retelling of his story here.

CHAPTER 3:

EGYPTIAN MYTHOLOGY

WHO WERE THE EGYPTIANS?

The Ancient Egyptians unified as a single civilization along the banks of the life-bringing River Nile in c. 3150 BC. The mythical King Meni was charged with unifying what is now known as Upper and Lower Egypt almost overnight, but the truth is it took much longer for diplomatic developments to reach conclusion – but myth, as ever, prefers the simpler route. As the keen-eyed reader will note, this made the ancient Egyptians contemporaries of the nearby Sumerians (see Chapter 2).

We can all of us conjure up an image of Ancient Egypt: mummified dead, pyramids, hieroglyphics, pharaohs and the Sphinx, which illustrates how deeply embedded Egyptian culture was with ritual, religion, myth and a wonderfully unique identity. The Egyptian land and culture reached its peak from c. 1500 to 1000 BC, and it is during this time that the divine pharaohs (about whom we learnt at school) ruled – Hatshepsut, Ramesses the Great and Tutenkhamun, to name but a few.

In the fourth century BC, Alexander III of Macedon, better known as the Greek leader Alexander the Great, conquered the enormous Persian Empire, commandeering a vast swathe of territories that included Syria and Egypt. Over the next eight years, the leader of the Greeks would go on to create an empire that straddled three continents. In Egypt, Alexander founded Alexandria, a new capital city, which still bears the same name to this day. But even in the face of such defeat, the religion and myths of the Ancient Egyptians were barely disturbed and there followed an exchange of wisdom and science between the Greeks and the Egyptians, with Alexandria heralded as a famous seat of learning.

Egyptian mythology was complex, influenced not only by the country's geography, with the Nile at its heart and surrounded by the sea, mountains and desert, but also by its longevity as a civilization. Eighteen successive royal dynasties spanning an extraordinary 2,500 years influenced heavily the culture and religious attitude of ancient Egypt. And for the Egyptians, myths were more than just stories. While the ancient tales of the Egyptian gods had their root in the few certainties of the universe – such as the passage of the sun, moon and stars – they also sought to help with lessons of morality and conduct in contemporary society.

The Creation of
the Universe

There is more than one account of Egyptian creation because, it seems, the different regions that made up the culture each wanted to impose their local deities and aetiological legends on to the ancient stories, and so the names and details vary depending on the story. (The Egyptians later reconciled this with a relenting acknowledgement that inventing the whole universe probably took the work of a number of different deities, all of whom, coincidentally, decided to do so on the same day.)

In the beginning (of one story, at least), there was nothing but a nebulous chaos of nothingness, personified by the god Nun. From this emptiness emerged a pyramidal mound known as Ben-Ben, upon which the creator Atum emerged from a lotus flower, bringing with him light. (It is for this reason that Atum is also closely associated with the sun god Ra.) Atum produced the first generation of gods by masturbating into the void and bringing forth Shu, the god of air, and Tefnut, the goddess of rain and moisture. These two gods in turn procreated, giving birth to Geb, the god of the earth, and Nut, the goddess of the sky, with her father, Shu, lifting up his daughter so she could arch over her brother Geb as a canopy of stars.

Following the creation of the earth, sky and the air between it, Atum ruled over the Egyptian universe as the first ever pharaoh. And, having caught wind of a prophecy that the goddess of the sky, Nut, would give birth to a child that would overthrow him, Atum forbade her from doing so. Unfortunately, Nut failed to oblige and she gave birth to four children: Osiris, Isis, Set and Nephthys – the first of whom grew up to fulfil the prophecy. (The Greeks had a very similar myth in Cronos' struggle for power – see page 144.)

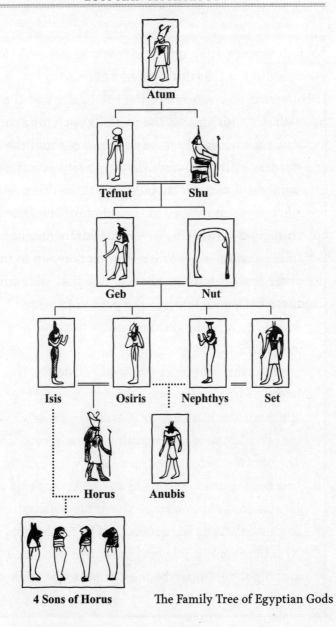

Atum

Tefnut **Shu**

Geb **Nut**

Isis **Osiris** **Nephthys** **Set**

Horus **Anubis**

4 Sons of Horus The Family Tree of Egyptian Gods

Heart vs Ma'at

When Atum created the world, the chaos and disorder of Nun was pushed out beyond the borders of the universe. In its place was left a wonderful sense of balance, justice and cosmic harmony, known as Ma'at. This principle of universal truth was present in all elements of Egyptian life, informing their morality, their understanding of cosmology, as well as their laws and politics. The personification of Ma'at was a young goddess, often seen wearing a feather.

Egyptians thought the soul resides in the heart. When an Egyptian died, Anubis (god of the dead) would take their heart and place it on a set of scales, weighing it against Ma'at's feather. The outcome determined how closely the person had lived their life according to Ma'at principles. Hearts that did not make the grade suffered a second death and were consumed by the goddess Ammit – a hungry hybrid of lioness, crocodile and hippopotamus (the most frightening man-eating creatures known to the Egyptians) – and their bodies were condemned to an eternity in the underworld, known as Duat. Those whose hearts balanced on the scales with Ma'at's feather faced a far more pleasant outcome: they were sent on to everlasting paradise in Aaru.

The pharaohs that ruled Egypt were said to be of direct lineage from the gods, and their key role in leadership was thus to uphold the principles of Ma'at. One way to maintain the cosmic balance was through rituals, myth and ceremony in the name of the gods and the pharaohs – and so it was for this constant affirmation of Ma'at that the Egyptians created such a rich compendium of customs.

The Resurrection of Osiris

Osiris, who from birth was destined to overthrow Atum to become the ruler of the Egyptian universe, hailed from a close-knit family. He united with his sister Isis, while his brother, Set, formed a union with their other sister Nephthys. However, not content with just one sisterly union, Osiris also embarked on a dalliance with his other sister (and sister-in-law), Nephthys, the result of which was Anubis, the embalming god of the dead.

Angry at this breach of trust, Set jealously murdered his brother, an event which came to represent the constant struggle between order and disorder under the Egyptian principle of Ma'at. The exact details of the murder are sparsely recorded as the Egyptians gave great significance to their hieroglyphic writing and thought it capable of bringing to reality any destructive things that were written down.

Isis and Nephthys went in search of Osiris' body, and Isis' tears of grief as she searched in vain for her husband and brother gave rise to the idea that they caused the flooding of the Nile each year (and which is why Osiris is seen as bringing life and fertility to the region). With the help of Anubis (funerary god), Isis and Nephthys recovered their brother's body and embalmed it to bring him back to life – a custom that was repeated on the dead throughout Ancient Egypt, with the hope of halting and even turning back the decomposition of the body after death.

However, Osiris' resurrection was only partial, since his subsequent role was as leader of the dead in Anubis' place. Granted only a few moments of life, Osiris took it as an opportunity to procreate with his wife Isis, which brought them a son, Horus.

Horus

The falcon-headed Horus was god of the sky, seen as a protector and a symbol of power, as well as the god of hunting and war. One of the most enduring symbols of Egyptian mythology is the Eye of Horus, which was used as an emblem for protection and guidance in jewellery and sculpture, as well as painted onto the bows of ships. Horus' eyes were said to resemble the sun (personified in the sun god Ra) and the moon (personified in the moon god Thoth). All-seeing eyes are important symbols not only for the Egyptians; similar icons are present in the Christian Eye of Providence, on the back of the US dollar bill and – of course – in the Eye of Sauron in *The Lord of the Rings*.

The Eye of Horus

Following Set's murder of Osiris, he and Horus engaged in an ongoing struggle for power, and a variety of myths tell of the numerous fights, challenges and trickery that ensued between the two gods. One such story sees Horus take a testicle from Set. Another witnesses Set gouging out one of Horus' eyes. In yet another myth, Set tries to impregnate Horus with his 'seed' – considered by the Egyptians to be both a potent poison and a degrading abuse of power. Horus is able to catch the semen in his hands and throw it into the river, and wreaks revenge when he plants his own semen onto a lettuce leaf that Set then eats, thus ending in his defeat.

Despite the violent nature of these stories, they fulfilled an allegorical role. Set is often seen as the god of Upper Egypt (towards the source of the Nile), and Horus the god of Lower Egypt (around the Nile Delta) and their conflict represents not only the struggle between order and disorder to maintain the all-important Ma'at (see page 58), but also the unification of these two lands in the late fourth millennium BC into one country.

Lower Egypt, which includes the fertile and life-giving Nile Delta (and today the cities of Cairo and Alexandria), was dominant over Upper Egypt when the two regions merged into one, and the removal of one of Set's testicles gave rise to the reason why the region of Upper Egypt remained a dry and unfertile desert. The gouging out and later restoration of Horus' left eye (associated with the moon) explains why the night sky goes dark once every month before the moon returns to its visible orbit.

The Wonders of the Ancient World

The oldest-surviving pyramid-shaped structure dates back to around 2600 BC, and ancient Egypt seems to have been littered with such edifices, with well over 100 uncovered by archaeologists to date. The pharaohs of Egypt were considered direct descendants of the gods, and indeed as Horus in human form, and as such were given due pomp and ceremony in their death. Their bodies were embalmed in the belief that this would reverse the decomposition process, and they were buried inside the stone pyramids.

The shape of the structures offered steps up to the heavens, and were originally clad in brilliant polished limestone casing stones, giving them a bright white reflective shine that must have been phenomenal to behold. Their shape was said to mimic that of Ben-Ben, the original mound of the Egyptian universe, from which everything else was created (see page 55).

In some pyramids, the bodies were buried below ground level with all manner of riches, and, in the case of the Great Pyramid at Giza, the artefacts include an entire wooden boat stored in pieces alongside the dead. This largest and most famous of all the pyramids once stood an incredible 146 metres tall (the equivalent of a forty-four-storey building). Its secret chambers are still being discovered today, and the deliberately perplexing corridors within the pyramids have given rise to the captivating mysticism of Ancient Egypt.

CHAPTER 4:

CHINESE MYTHOLOGY

ANCIENT CHINA

As an ancient culture, Chinese mythology has been influenced by many religious and cultural belief systems. The stories of Chinese mythology have been around for thousands of years and they tell of the beginnings of the Chinese people, of their legendary leaders, and of the development of customs and religion. The earliest examples of Chinese writing still in existence are carved onto bone fragments that date back to c. 1200 BC. However, it is estimated that the earliest ruling dynasty emerged approximately one thousand years before this, from 2100 BC, when the Xia dynasty is thought to have ruled along the Yellow River valley, which means the stories and beliefs that define this civilization would have arisen from as early as this time.

From around 485 BC, China was divided into several competing states, out of which rose the Qin dynasty in 221 BC, which formed China's first united empire. Although the Qin dynasty lasted until only 207 BC, it established the approximate boundaries and basic administrative systems that are still a feature of modern-day China. And from such early beginnings, China has grown to become the largest country in the world – with one-fifth of the world's population and a staggering 1.3 billion people falling under its jurisdiction.

Bai She Zhuan
(The White Snake Woman)

The legend of the white snake woman, which tells of the spirits of a white snake and a green snake, who live in the West Lake of Hangzhou, has been in existence for hundreds of years. It has been the subject of many Chinese plays, novels, operas and, even, movies and computer games, and, as such, many different versions of it are told.

The white snake, now known as Bai She Zhuan, and the green snake, known as Xiaoqing, practised Taoist magic in a quest for immortality, and eventually possessed enough power to transform themselves into beautiful women. Bai She Zhuan then met a young man called Xu Xian by the broken bridge of the lake and the two fell in love after he offered her an umbrella in the rain; they eventually married and opened up a pharmacy in a nearby town. But Xu Xian later met a Buddhist monk called Fa Hai, who could sense Xu Xian's new bride was in fact a snake, and he warned him against her. During an annual Dragon Boat Festival, Fa Hai then tricked Xu Xian into giving his wife some arsenic. Pregnant with her first child, Bai She Zhuan's magical powers were weakened, and she could not help but reveal her true form as a white snake. Xu Xian promptly dropped down dead with shock.

Revived with a special herb, Xu Xian's luck quickly came to an end when he was forcibly separated from his wife by Fa Hai and locked in a temple. Bai She Zhuan attempted to rescue her imprisoned husband by flooding the temple in the hope it would flush out Fa Hai. A struggle ensued, but the green snake, Xiaoqing, came to the rescue and helped Bai She Zhuan and Xu Xian to overcome their adversary. The lovers were temporarily reunited at the broken bridge, until Bai She Zhuan gave birth to their son, after which she was captured by Fa Hai and imprisoned in the Lei Feng Pagoda.

Many years later, the green snake returned to free Bai She Zhuan from jail, by which point her son had grown up to become a Chinese civil servant. The end of the story varies, but one version sees Bai She Zhuan granted immortality but eternal separation from her husband and son, and her spirit can still be seen, apparently, on the long, low broken bridge when it is covered in snow.

Analyses of this story vary according to which adaptation you read, but the idea behind this particular version is the triumph of social morality over individual desire. It was deemed improper for the snake and the young man to fall in love, and it was against the will of the wise monk, hence their punishment. Conversely, the behaviour of the couple that was deemed proper is celebrated: they work hard on a noble business, and their son gets a good education and remains loyal to his father. And it is only once their son has achieved social success that Bai She Zhuan is freed from her prison to return to the west lake.

Kua Fu

Kua Fu was the leader of a group of giants, and his story is one of the oldest Chinese fables. It acts as an aetiological tale for the origins of a variety of geological features, as well as teaching us the importance of humility.

During one particularly hot summer, when the land was parched and the forest was scorched, the giants found themselves too exhausted to move. In an effort to cool things down, Kua Fu vowed that he would chase the sun along its course to capture and tame it. He ran as fast as he could across the land for nine days and nine nights and as he went he brushed off the dust from his sandals, which then formed the large hills on the landscape. He also created three huge mountains from the three stones that held his cooking pot at night.

When Kua Fu finally caught up with the sun, its heat was too much to bear, so he ran to the Yellow River to try in vain to quench his thirst. Still parched, he drank instead from the Wei River – but this failed too to satisfy his thirst. In a desperate final attempt to succeed, Kua Fu headed for the Great Lake – but alas, it was all too much for him and he dropped dead gasping for water.

His story serves to remind us of the importance of leadership, but acts as a very clear warning of the dangers of arrogance. Interestingly, the hero who becomes weaker the closer he gets to the sun can also be seen in the Greek myth of Icarus (see page 166).

ANIMALS AND CREATURES

Like the other stories examined in this book, monsters and other creatures play an important part in Chinese mythology.

Dragons

One of the most recognizable Chinese symbols is the dragon, seen variously today in the long, snaking puppet of Chinese festivals, in the designs of many Chinese-inspired buildings around the globe, and, of course, in the names of many of our favourite Chinese restaurants. Far from the fire-breathing maiden-snatcher of British legend, the Chinese dragon is a benevolent and auspicious creature, whose graceful flight and magical abilities make it a revered augur of prosperity. It is a hybrid of several animals (a tiger's paws, the eyes of a hare, the horns of a stag, the scales of a carp, and so on), all of which results in a creature that is said to be a sign of great power and prosperity. Ancient leaders would even associate themselves with the dragon to show their authority.

Despite the Western association of dragons with fire breathing, Chinese dragons are associated with moisture, rain and clouds. Their breath is said to produce clouds, their swirling flight to generate storms, and their wrath can bring both floods and drought, depending on their whim. They are the guardians of the weather, the seasons, and even of the passing of night and day.

In art, sculpture and ornaments, the Chinese dragon is often seen clutching or reaching out for a pearl. This represents a very enigmatic truth or wisdom that the dragon is striving for; it symbolizes the very energy (or chi) that brings all things into balance and is the universal progenitor of all things. Sometimes the ball is even depicted as the globe itself.

Chinese
New Year

More than just a celebration of the passing of time, Chinese New Year also commemorates a powerful mythological story.

In ancient times, Nian ('the year') was a ghastly monster who indulged his passion for eating people every New Year's Eve. And so, each New Year the people would flee their villages and go into hiding into the mountains until the marauding beast had gone.

One year, an old beggar came ambling into a village just as the inhabitants were making their annual flight. He pleaded with one old woman to let him stay in her home for the evening. She explained their yearly horror, and advised him strongly to join them in the mountains. But he was not to be moved; he swore that in exchange for one night's accommodation, he would fight off the hungry Nian.

When finally, at midnight, Nian entered the village in search of his next meal, he was startled by what he saw. In front of him, the old woman's house was daubed in red paint and surrounded by burning fires and the air was ringing out with the crash and bang of exploding firecrackers. At that moment, the front door of the old woman's house was flung open to reveal the old beggar dressed in a red robe and surrounded by the bright lights of his fires. Alarmed by this spectacle, Nian fled the village in fear.

Even today, the people of China stay up all night on New Year's Eve to light fires, set off fireworks and decorate their homes in red to ward off the terrible beast.

The Chinese Zodiac

Like many other cultures, the ancient Chinese people associated certain astrological phenomena with different aspects of an individual's personality. Each year of the Chinese calendar was linked to a different animal, twelve in total, each of whom possessed its own characteristics that are then transferred onto the people born in that year. The same animals were also used to denote the time of the day (in twelve two-hour chunks).

1936, 1948, 1960, 1972, 1984, 1996, 2008

Rat people are quick-witted, popular and funny. They are very loyal and up for a challenge, but can be motivated by money and greed.

1937, 1949, 1961, 1973, 1985, 1997, 2009

Ox people are dependable, strong-willed and good leaders. They are prone to stubbornness and can sometimes feel isolated.

1938, 1950, 1962, 1974, 1986, 1998, 2010

Tiger people are calm and authoritative leaders. They are ambitious, courageous and philosophical, but can be moody and intense, too. Watch out for the claws.

1939, 1951, 1963, 1975, 1987, 1999, 2011

Rabbit people are homebodies who like to be surrounded by family and friends. They are genuine in personality, very trustworthy and will avoid conflict at all costs – which may make them easy prey.

1940, 1952, 1964, 1976, 1988, 2000, 2012

Dragon people are very lucky – this is one of the most powerful Chinese signs. They are natural leaders and have bags of personality, but will do anything to get to the top.

1941, 1953, 1965, 1977, 1989, 2001, 2013

Snake people are an intelligent bunch. They are good with money, seductive and charming. They may be prone to jealousy and have a slightly dangerous edge.

1942, 1954, 1966, 1978, 1990, 2002, 2014

Horse people are hard-working self-starters who are charming but impatient. They love to travel, but this can also come across as being transient.

1943, 1955, 1967, 1979, 1991, 2003, 2015

Goat people are creative beings. Their mind can wander off into its own little world – making them great thinkers and philosophers, but also disposed to anxieties and insecurities and in need of reassurance.

1944, 1956, 1968, 1980, 1992, 2004, 2016

Monkey people are energetic and lively. They are good listeners, but live in the moment and look after their own interests first. They are fun to be around, but may struggle with long-term commitment.

1945, 1957, 1969, 1981, 1993, 2005, 2017

Rooster people are straightforward, practical and think deeply. They are perfectionists and hard-working, which may sometimes come across as being a bit too neat and tidy.

1946, 1958, 1970, 1982, 1994, 2006, 2018

Dog people are trustworthy and honest. They do well in business, but aren't shy of telling the odd lie or having the occasional mood swing.

1947, 1959, 1971, 1983, 1995, 2007, 2019

Pig people are great companions, and enjoy helping others. They have impeccable taste and are inquisitive. They always get a job done and are intelligent. But don't test them – they will react.

CHAPTER 5:

AMERICAN
INDIAN
MYTHOLOGY

WHO WERE THE
AMERICAN INDIANS?

The date of the first human migrations to North America is a hotly debated topic, but the continent has been inhabited from at least 10,000 BC, if not very much longer before that. These new inhabitants spread themselves across both North and South America over time, with different civilizations flourishing at different times. The emergence of a culture that we would now associate with American Indians can be seen in the northern continent between around 1000 BC and AD 1000, the later date by which the Mississippian culture had developed the huge city of Cahokia. Situated in what is modern-day St Louis, Missouri, Cahokia reached a population of up to 20,000 people – matching contemporary London in size.

American Indian culture is centred on a deep spiritual balance with nature, and is intrinsically linked with the land. Animals play a huge part in their mythology: all living things are seen to possess an individual spirit, as well as belonging to the collective spirit of the world. They view their land as belonging to all creatures, and hunters would thank the spirits of the animals they killed for food.

European explorers arrived in America from 1492 onwards, bringing with them, amongst other gifts, disease and colonialism – neither of which made for favourable living conditions. The population of American Indians nosedived in the centuries that followed, in a cultural clash that is still fraught today.

SPIRITS AND RITUALS

The creation myths of the American Indians are as varied as the number of tribes that populated North America. At the point of the arrival of Europeans in 1492, there could have been ten million people or more inhabiting the area that is now the USA, forming over 500 distinct tribal groups. With such figures it is possible to see how diverse the different philosophies could be across one continent.

Wakan Tanka and
the Creation

Despite these discrepancies, the Sioux and Lakota tribes shared similar belief systems and customs, which focused on an entity known as Wakan Tanka, which is sometimes translated as 'the Great Mystery' or 'the Great Spirit', and which represents the universal spirit in all things. It is thought that, in the time before anything existed, Wakan Tanka was in a nebulous dark void called Han. The first entity came in the form of Inyan, the rock, who poured out his energy in the form of the blue blood of the seas and created the earth goddess Maka from himself.

In creating Maka, Inyan had given her the elements of discord and negativity (among other things, of course). As such, she started to complain, her biggest gripe being that she was created from Inyan and was not, therefore, her own entity. She was also upset that she was still living in the darkness of Han and so was unable to see a reflection of herself. The third god was Skan, the sky god. Being more spirit than the physical Inyan and Maka, he assumed a much more divine role. He acted as a judge of all things, and so listened to Maka's concerns.

To placate her, Skan decreed that Han should be split in two, dividing her between the upper world, where she was personified as Anp and would exist in light, and below the earth as Han, where she would continue to live in darkness.

In the upper world, Maka saw how beautiful the blue oceans were and how bare she looked, so she took some of the water and wore lakes and rivers as trinkets to make herself feel pretty. Not content, Maka continued to complain, which resulted in Skan creating the fourth primordial god, Wi, whom he placed in the sky to shine light over the earth. He declared that Wi should provide heat, and should cast shadows on all things – which was thought to represent the inseparable individual spirits of all entities – and instructed Anp and Han to share the sky as night and day.

The Importance of Circles

For many American Indians, the circle is the most sacred of shapes as it is present in all things, both literally and metaphorically, and prevalent in a variety of rituals. From the dome of the sky and the shape of the earth – it is possible to see circles in everything.

As such, circles are significant in American Indian customs, and huge circular stone structures can be seen laid on the ground across the USA for use during ceremonies. These 'medicine circles' consist of a central stone from which four small lines of stones point out in the opposite directions of the compass. Each line of stones is associated with a different colour, element, animal and life stage. (The Aztecs also associated the four directions with colours, and their gods were made up of different-coloured elements, each of which was associated with a particular direction.)

The Sun Dance and the Ghost Dance

Performed in the summer to provide a successful bison hunt and to replenish the animal population for the future, the sun dance ritual was an annual ceremony steeped in spiritual significance. During the ceremony, the men of the tribe sat in a specially built structure which had an opening to the sky and a tall tree in its centre, upon which was placed a bison skull.

The young men would paint their bodies yellow, wear decorative feathers and take part in several days of fasting, self-harm and ritual, with the intention of becoming unconscious in order to receive spiritual visitations. The ceremony would culminate with the men attaching cords from the top of the pole to their nipples and performing a dance.

Such activities did not sit well with the Christian sensibilities of white Americans, and the practice was forcibly suppressed. However, it did not die out entirely and soon took on another form as the ghost dance. Popularized in 1889 by an American Indian prophet known as Wovoka, the dance was said to bring the participants closer to the spirits of the dead. In a time when the clash between old and new America was reaching its peak, the dance was carried out to bring unity and balance back to the land and to return the continent to its pre-invasion status.

However, the widespread practice of the dance had the opposite effect. The US military arrested and even killed American Indian leaders who failed to prevent their tribes from performing it – and one attack on a camp in Wounded Knee Creek, South Dakota, in 1890 ended in the massacre of more than 150 American Indians. The dead included many women and children, and they were buried unceremoniously in a mass grave.

American Indian Words in Modern Culture

Approximately half the states that make up the USA are named after Native American words or tribes from that region. There are also many everyday words in modern English that have their roots in the languages spoken across the pre-Columbian Americas (north and south), including barbecue, hurricane, tomato, potato, cocaine, moose, racoon and toboggan, to name just a few. Beyond these direct translations into English, we have also adopted American Indian terms to use in our own (commercial) culture to evoke some of the heroism and mysticism of their native myths.

It is undeniable that most of the uses of these terms for commercial benefit are a somewhat narrow-sighted attempt to evoke images of manly, outdoorsy warrior types, and they do not represent the full picture of the hundreds of different tribes that inhabited the continent. It seems we have bought into our own myth of what it is to be a Native American and continue to perpetuate a stereotype.

	What we think it is	What it really is
Apache	A type of Jeep for off-roading with your friends.	A conglomeration of various tribes from the south-west of the United States.
Cherokee	Another type of Jeep. These days more likely to see a supermarket car park than a precipitous dirt track.	A tribe situated in the south-east of the USA.
Chinook	A military helicopter with two rotors.	A group of tribes situated in the Pacific north-west of the USA.
Mohawk	A hairstyle popularized by the punks of 1980s Britain, often dyed.	A tribe from what is now upstate New York. While they did have rather fancy hair, the modern 'Mohawk' style is closer in cut to that of the Pawnee tribe in today's Nebraska.
Pocahontas	A Disney princess. She falls in love with Englishman John Smith and saves him from execution by the American Indians.	In reality, that's just where the story begins. In the early seventeenth century, Pocahontas married another Englishman after the John Smith incident, in what is thought to be the first interracial marriage in America. She converted to Christianity and moved to London as something of a celebrity, where she died at the tender age of twenty-two from a ghastly disease.

	What we think it is	What it really is
Tomahawk	A long-range cruise missile.	The traditional axe with a head made from sharpened flint or antlers. Some ingenious people even carved a hollow out of the handle so the tool could double up as a pipe.
Quahog	The fictional town in Rhode Island made famous by American animated series *Family Guy*.	A round, hard-shelled clam found on the Atlantic coast. The name comes from the Narraganset language, and is short for poquauhock (from pohkeni 'dark' + hogki 'shell').
Winnebago	Huge mobile homes for cross-continent road trips and touring rock bands alike.	A tribe now residing in Nebraska.

The Myths of the Plains

The plains covered what is now the Midwest and the south of the USA and the mythological stories associated with this area held important lessons for the American Indians.

The White Buffalo Woman

Several tribes of the plains tell the myth of the White Buffalo Woman, known as Pteskawin. She acts as a bringer of rituals to these tribes – a role personified by many civilizations the world over to give significance to the customs that are continued in the name of spirituality.

In a time when food was scarce, two young hunters left their tribe before dawn in search of prey. They wandered far and yet found no animals that they could bring back to feed their people. After a long search, they reached the top of a hill and looked out across the prairie, where they spotted something bright coming towards them from the horizon – which, as it approached, turned out to be Pteskawin, a beautiful woman wearing a brilliant-white hide. Understandably taken by the beauty of this unexpected apparition, one of the young hunters approached her with amorous intent. His companion could see that she was wakan (or holy), and urged his naive friend to respect her spirituality. But it was too late: as the woman embraced the young man, a cloud enveloped them both and disappeared to reveal nothing but bones lying at her feet.

Now that she had her audience's attention, the woman instructed the remaining hunter to go back to his tribe and tell the chief to gather all his people under one tepee for her imminent arrival. Obediently, the hunter ran back at once and a huge tepee was built for all the tribe, in which they all waited in respectful anticipation of her dramatic entrance.

Pteskawin entered the tepee, walked around its circumference following the direction of the sun and stood before the chief on the west side. She gave him the sacred chanunpa (smoking pipe), which was carved with symbols representing the earth, the buffalo, the forest and the birds. It acted as the tool for several important rituals for these tribes, and the smoking of it brought tribesmen closer to the spiritual world.

As she left, Pteskawin was seen to turn into a buffalo, bow to the four directions of the earth and disappear into the horizon. Many of the actions described in the myth continue to be important elements of American Indian culture, particularly for the Lakota tribe from where the story originates: the various uses and meanings of the pipe, the communal lodge, the following of the direction of the sun and the historical importance of the buffalo as a resource.

The Wily Coyote

The cartoon coyote of the same name is inspired by an ancient American Indian myth of the Lakota tribe. In the more traditional version, this trickster was wandering across the plains with his friend Iktome, the spider spirit, when they came across a huge rock. Coyote recognized great soul and life in the rock and saw that it was the spirit Iya.

Coyote took off the blanket he was wearing and placed it over the rock to keep it warm, and the two friends continued on their way. Later on, it started to rain and become cold, and the adventurers sought shelter in a damp cave, where Iktome remained warm under his thick hide and Coyote regretted his earlier generosity. Suddenly recalibrating his morality, Coyote determined that an old rock had no need for a blanket and demanded that Iktome go back to retrieve it. After the spider's unsuccessful attempt, it was left to Coyote to go shivering back and yank the hide from the rock's back himself.

Content, the two companions continued on their journey. However, when they came to rest once again in another cave they heard a distant rumble. The noise was getting louder by the minute as it resonated across the plain and echoed in the cave behind them. Suddenly on the horizon they could see the great rock Iya rolling towards them, crushing everything in its path, clearly making his way to Coyote.

Petrified, Wily and Iktome fled. They tried several techniques to outwit Iya – swimming across the river and weaving in and out of the forest – but to no avail: the rock continued to roll at speed towards them. It was only Iktome who was able to outwit the rock by rolling himself into a ball and disappearing down a tiny hole. The poor coyote, on the other hand, was flattened by the rock.

This is another legend that punishes the disregard of sacred things, and is an illustration of spirit that American Indians saw in all creatures and objects of the earth. They had no temples or shrines – the spirituality of their belief system was alive in all things. Moreover, Iya was seen as a storm god, so the story helps to give explanation to the destructive nature of hurricanes, punishing the sins of Coyote (to use Christian terminology). It also gives us an insight into the morality of the tribe that told this tale: it beseeches the listener to keep their generosity genuine and is a reflection of the very fair and unquestioning kind-heartedness with which the Lakota wanted to treat their fellow tribesmen.

CHAPTER 6:

SOUTH AND CENTRAL AMERICAN MYTHOLOGY

THE MAYANS

The Mayans first emerged as a distinct civilization in *c.* 2000 BC and occupied a region in Central America now covered by Guatemala, Belize and parts of southern Mexico, as well as western Honduras and northern El Salvador. They reached their peak in *c.* AD 250, and eventually waned around AD 900, but their languages, mythologies and culture are still prevalent in the region today.

Much like the Greeks in their heyday (see Chapter 7), Mayan society was structured as a series of independent city-states, each with its own powerful king. They built wonderful temples and palaces, and are credited with having had the only known fully developed writing system in pre-Colombian America.

Mayan culture was thick with art, ceremony and tradition, and they were partial to human sacrifice too. The Mayans also had very advanced abilities in astronomy, mathematics and agriculture.

The End of the World (Or Not)

People the world over became excited by the ancient Mayan prediction that the world would end on 21 December 2012, reported in news bulletins across the globe with a slightly nervous tongue in cheek. Bugarach, a small mountain village in southern France, was rumoured to be one of the few places where people would be safe, and some people even bought one-way tickets to spend time with the bewildered locals.

The Mayans categorized dates using three different calendars. The Haab was the civil calendar and it counted 365 days in each cycle, with each year broken into nineteen months, each of which consisted of twenty days, except for one month of just five days. The Tzolk'in was the divine calendar that dictated the dates of religious ceremonies; it counted 260 days in each cycle, which were subdivided into twenty sections of thirteen days each. The final calendar was the Long Count, which was an astronomical calendar consisting of approximately 7,885 years in each cycle. At the end of each cycle, the world would end and be reborn.

Over the years, keen conspiracy theorists worked

out that the end of the latest Long Count cycle would fall on 21 December 2012. Although the Mayans did not predict anything too ghastly – it was just the end of one calendar and the beginning of another, much like we experience each 1 January – worry spread that the end of the world was nigh.

Bugarach's association with the debacle was somewhat absurd. What began as spurious Internet-based rumour-mongering, naming the village as a safe haven from the impending apocalypse, quickly transformed into something much bigger. The region's mayor dared to mention the village's safe-haven status in a council meeting in the years running up to Armageddon, which was soon picked up by local newspapers. Once it began to be reported on news networks across the globe, the association was complete.

This story illustrates the sheer power of myths and storytelling. Even those people who joked about the end of the world still had an uneasy look in their eyes, and those who relocated to France (despite never having heard of Mayan theology before) illustrated how far we are still from understanding the world around us – and how readily we will cling to any elaborate story that seeks to make sense of it.

The Mayan Calendar

The World Tree

The concept of a World Tree is a tradition central to many world mythologies (see page 196 for the Norse interpretation). According to the Mayans, the World Tree (Wacah Chan) formed the very basis of the universe, and was anchored in the Mayan people's astrological observations of the Milky Way, which seemed to grow up into the heavens from the horizon. The roots of the World Tree were based deep down in the underworld (Xibalba), its trunk in the middle, mortal world, and its celestial branches stretching out into the heavens. The trunk of the tree was sometimes seen to be formed from reptilian creatures.

The name Wacah Chan means 'erect serpent', and it describes the bright, straight line of the Milky Way as it emerged from the horizon at certain times of the year. The tree reached out in the four directions in the mortal world, and worked as a reassuring visualization for the Mayan people: the sturdy strength of the tree represented the strong core at both the centre of all humans and the centre of each important ritual, stretching out in all directions, connecting all mortals and all gods.

The Mayan World Tree

Itzamná

God of creation, inventor of writing and the calendar, Itzamná was generous-spirited and married to the rather more mean-natured goddess Ixchel, who filled her palace with vats of water which she would rain down on the worlds below causing huge storms and floods. Itzamná was the leader of the gods, whom he presided over from his throne, and he became the patron deity of medicine, as well as bringing culture, rituals and knowledge to the Mayan people. Sometimes, he was depicted as four gods (the Itzamnás), each pertaining to one of the four main compass points.

Itzamná was, according to different sources, either the son of or the visible incarnation of Hanab Ku – the abstract spirit from which everything else came. One myth tells how Hanab Ku created and recreated three sets of mortals in the world before he reached a state of happiness. He destroyed his first creation, the little people, with the help of a water-spewing serpent after he discovered they were not to his liking; his second attempt generated a people known as the Dzolob, whom he too destroyed with a flood after deciding they were not quite right; finally he created the Mayans, by which point he was, thankfully, content.

The physical manifestation of Hanab Ku's spirit in

Itzamná was an elderly man with an enormous hooked nose. He was a benevolent patriarch that protected the Mayan people, who often held ceremonies in his honour at the transition into a new calendar cycle to bring prosperity and health.

Chac

As the god of rain, Chac became an increasingly important figure in Mayan religious ceremonies and human sacrifices. With sharp fangs, huge goggling eyes that shed tears of rain, a snout-like nose, a reptilian body and carrying a serpent axe that represented the lightning bolts for which he was known, Chac cut a distinctive figure. Like the other major Mayan gods, Chac possessed four different personalities, each of which was associated with the four points of a compass, called the Chacs (the name also given to the four priests who would hold down each limb of a sacrificial victim).

In the very beginning of time, Chac split open a sacred rock with his axe, from which sprang the very first ear of corn. He subsequently taught the Mayans agriculture and kept control of water in the atmosphere as well as on the ground, which meant he was held in very high esteem. Chac was associated with frogs, since they signalled the coming of rain, and part of religious ceremonies in his honour would require four young men to impersonate frogs.

The Hero Twins

Hunahpu and Xbalanque were a sprightly set of twins skilled particularly at ball games. So noisy were they about their victories that even the Lords of Death in the underworld (Xibalba) caught wind of their prowess. Having cleanly dispatched the twins' father and uncle, who had themselves been a boastful pair of ball-playing twins only one generation previously, the Lords were somewhat perturbed by current proceedings. They summoned the boys to the underworld.

The twins were subjected to a set of challenges similar to those their father and uncle had faced. They managed successfully to outsmart the Lords' first trick: having disguised themselves as wooden carvings, the Lords tried to force their guests to sit on a burning bench, but the twins, realizing the seat was hot, refused. The challenges continued. Hunahpu and Xbalanque were handed a flaming torch and cigar each and instructed to keep them burning until the following day. They managed to trick the Lords by tying fireflies to the ends of the cigars and replacing the torch flame with the bright-red tail of a macaw, which gave the illusion that the embers were still burning.

Hunahpu and Xbalanque continued to trick the Lords in a succession of further challenges – the most impressive of which saw Hunapu survive decapitation during a ball game by replacing his head with a squash fruit. However, realizing that their luck would no doubt soon run out, the twins accepted one final, fateful invitation from the Lords to step inside a fiery furnace, and to their deaths. But the twins were one day able to exact their revenge.

The Lords of Death ground up Hunapu and Xbalanque's bones and sprinkled them into a river, from which they were both reincarnated into several forms. The last of these transformations was into two travelling magicians, who were so skilled in their art they could perform human sacrifices and then reverse the process and bring the victims back to life.

The Lords of Death heard of their magical powers and requested a private showing in the depths of the underworld. So impressed were they by the twins' extraordinary death-reversal abilities, the Lords asked them to perform the trick on some of them. However, the boys, quite understandably, refused to undertake the resurrection part of the trick after they had performed the initial sacrifice. The glory days of Xibalba were brought to a close, and Hunapu and Xbalanque were raised into the sky to take on the forms of the sun and the moon.

THE AZTECS

An itinerant Mexica people united by the Nahuatl language, the Aztecs first occupied the region of central Mexico in the sixth century AD. A turbulent few centuries passed before they finally settled in 1325, when they founded the city of Tenochtitlán, a city-state situated on an island in Lake Texcoco. In 1427, a triple alliance of three Nahua city-states was formed when Tenochtitlán joined forces with Texcoco and Tlacopan, which signified the true unification of an Aztec people. Tenochtitlán acted as the centre of the Aztec Empire until the Spanish conquistadors destroyed it in the sixteenth century. The site of this ancient city is at the heart of where Mexico City stands today.

The itinerant past of the Mexica people gave rise to a mythical fatherland known as Aztlan, from where they had originated (hence the collective noun 'Aztec'), but the site – and existence – of this mythical land has been disputed.

The Aztec Creation Myth

The Aztecs believed it took several attempts to create the world before getting it right; each failed attempt gave rise to the creation of different creatures. In the beginning was Ometeotl, the very first god of all things. He bore four children, the Tezcatlipocas, each of whom was associated with a point on the compass.

In the first attempt, the earth was inhabited by berry-eating giants. The northern son of Ometeotl was known as the Black Tezcatlipoca, god of discord, light and beauty (among other things). He transformed himself into the sun and looked out over the world. His rival personality in the west was Quetzalcoatl, god of light and wind, who battled with his brother in the north and knocked him out of the sky. In retaliation, Black Tezcatlipoca returned as a jaguar and destroyed the world.

The second attempt at creation came when Quetzalcoatl was ruling the heavens. The people he produced on earth had a fondness for pine nuts, which meant that when Black Tezcatlipoca came down and wreaked yet more revenge, when he came as a wind to destroy everything, the few people who were left were turned into monkeys.

In the third attempt, Tlaloc, god of rain, took his turn as the sun, but this time Quetzalcoatl sent down rain that flooded the earth and destroyed everything again. The few people who remained were turned into birds to escape the deluge. Chalchiuhtlicue, the goddess of water, was the fourth one to take on the role of the sun – but her attempts were also destroyed by a flood of her own tears of blood, with the few survivors turning into fish.

Finally, after three failed attempts to create the world, the four gods put their heads together to devise a solution.

Quetzalcoatl resolved to travel to the underworld and retrieve the crushed bones of all who had died, resurrecting them by mixing them with his own blood. According to Aztec mythology, all humans are descended from this fourth and final attempt at creation; the variations in shape and size a consequence of the differences in size of the fragments of bone.

This idea of destruction and rebirth can also be seen in Mayan mythology (see page 106), the Norse concept of Ragnarök (see page 212) and even in Noah's Ark of the Bible.

Tlaloc

Similar to the Mayan god Chac (see page 112), Tlaloc was the Aztecs' answer to the god of rain, fertility and agriculture; he was also of a similarly striking appearance, sporting a pair of goggling eyes and protruding fangs. As he had occupied such a pivotal role in controlling the rain, water and therefore supply of food, temples were erected in Tlaloc's name around the Valley of Mexico. He was also the recipient of notable rituals in his name – including the sacrifice of men and even children.

Be Still
My Beating Heart

Sacrifice was an integral part of Aztec society. Because the gods had sacrificed themselves in the creation of the world, the Aztec people felt indebted to them and offered their own blood as a sign of their subservience. Rituals would sometimes take the form of removing beating hearts from human bodies and offering them to the gods.

Black Tezcatlipoca

THE INCAS

The empire of the Incas was vast, stretching over 2,400 miles along the Andes in South America. The Incas emerged as a group in *c.* 1200 and reached their height in the fifteenth century, by which point they inhabited a region that covered much of what is now Chile, Peru and Ecuador, as well as parts of Colombia, Bolivia and Argentina. This made theirs the largest united empire in all of the Americas at the time.

The Inca belief system was centred on the sun, which was seen as the giver of life to all things. As such, it was the Incas' ancestral father in the sky, and its importance is reflected in many of their myths. The Incas used their mythology to claim their authority over other tribes.

Unfortunately for the Incas, the onset of the age of discovery in the sixteenth century severely inhibited further growth. Indeed, the European invasion of the Americas didn't bode too well for the longevity of indigenous cultures, and the Incas' turn came around 1526 with the arrival of the first Spanish explorers in the region. Their population was ravaged by disease and war – with the last Inca leader being captured and executed less than fifty years later.

A Familiar
Creation Story

The mythology of the Incas held many similarities with those of the region's other indigenous tribes. According to the Inca creation story, in the beginning there was darkness, until the creator god Kon-Tiki Viracocha arose from what is now Lake Titicaca and brought forth the sun god Inti alongside the moon and stars.

As the god of creation, Viracocha – and in scenes reminiscent of both the Mayan and Aztec stories of creation (and not unlike the Christian story of Moses) – was displeased with the first batch of beings on the earth and sent a flood to destroy them all. Some myths tell of these people being turned into monkeys, which is a fate found in Aztec culture, too.

Viracocha created the new human race by scattering pebbles across the land. He bestowed upon them language, clothes, skills and laws, and taught them to develop harmony and knowledge by disguising himself as a beggar and wandering about the land teaching them how to live. According to some accounts of the creation story, Viracocha was dissatisfied still by this second group of people and it is thought he will one day return

to Earth to redeem the human race or impose upon us
another flood.

The Origin
of Cuzco

The city of Cuzco lay at the centre of the Inca Empire,
situated at 3,400 metres above sea level in what is now
southern Peru. To reinforce the historic importance of
this great city, Inca mythology decreed that Cuzco, its
location and its rulers were all directly decreed from
the gods themselves. (See also the story of Aeneas and
Rome on page 174.)

According to one myth, the sun god Inti created the
first Incan man and father of the Incas, Manco Capac,
and the first Incan woman, Mamaoqlyo, Manco's sister
and wife. Inti gave Manco a golden staff, with which he
and his sister-wife set off on their task to found the Incan
capital. They travelled far and wide across the Andes in
search of the sacred site, and knew finally when they
had hit the right spot when the golden staff sank into

the ground. It was here they built a temple to Inti and taught their people about the sun god from whom they were all descended.

In truth, the city predates the Incas. Before the Incas acquired Cuzco for themselves in the thirteenth century it was in the hands of the Killke people, who had occupied the surrounding region since *c.* 900. The city grew quickly under the Incas, but it required a divine myth to give the site prehistoric significance and to exalt the Inca people to godly levels of importance.

The Lost City of Machu Picchu

We cannot explore the Inca civilization without taking a quick trip up the mountains to Machu Picchu, which remains today one of the most iconic images of South America, and one of the most captivating sites of the ancient world. Machu Picchu is a settlement not all that far from the city of Cuzco in modern-day Peru, and the mysticism surrounding its crumbling temples and domestic buildings derives from the fact that it was built some 2,400 metres above sea level on a peak in the Andes and lay there completely undiscovered until 1911. Given that it was built in *c.* 1450, and the entire region was the victim of a thorough ransacking by the Spanish explorers from the end of the sixteenth century, it is a wonder that no one discovered this lost site until the twentieth century.

Although theories vary as to the purpose of Machu Picchu – it is thought to have been primarily a sacred retreat built for two of the most powerful Inca leaders, but other theories suggest it housed a population of some 1,000 people across the city – it offers a unique glimpse into Inca life. It houses several distinct areas for sacred buildings, royal palaces, industry, residence and farming. We can see that they had very advanced techniques for step farming up the steep Andean slopes and they used aqueducts to carry water from miles around to irrigate the land.

CHAPTER 7:

GREEK
MYTHOLOGY

WHO WERE THE GREEKS?

The civilization of the Ancient Greeks straddled a vast period and brought us, among other contributions, philosophy, literature, drama, theatre, laws, democracy, architecture and Pythagoras' theorem. Excavations in Knossos, Crete, revealed a large palace dating from approximately 2200 BC, which has been suggested as the home of King Minos, the ruler of the Minoans. The era of the Mycenaeans followed from about 1600 BC to 1200 BC, and most of the epic poems of Homer and the Greek tragedies are based on events during this period. Thanks to the efforts of Alexander the Great in the fourth century BC, the Greek Empire reached its height, extending across present-day Turkey, Egypt, Israel, Iran and all the way to India.

Greek civilization really came into its own in the eighth century BC, when the Greek alphabet as we know it was introduced. The Greeks put their writing skills to immediate good use, setting down some of the most famous myths we know today. Homer, the most famous of the Greek poets, lived in eastern Greece at some point between 800 and 700 BC, and his two epic poems *The Iliad* and *The Odyssey* are widely recognized as the first written works in the Western world. Many of Homer's stories still influence books and movies today.

The Greeks were all the rage until they handed the baton (with some resistance) over to the Romans during the second and first centuries BC. But the Romans took so much inspiration from Greek civilization (and which they proceeded to spread across their own empire) that the Greek legacy extended far beyond its own borders. Indeed, Greek mythology can probably lay claim to having had the biggest influence on the modern Western world – we've all heard about the Cyclops, Zeus and Poseidon, to name but three.

Gods and Goddesses

The Greek gods were a vengeful and rampant bunch. There were lots of them, too many to mention here, so I've narrowed the focus to the Olympians, who were a group of twelve gods that ruled following the overthrow of the Titans. Eleven of the twelve gods resided on Mount Olympus; the twelfth god, Hades, was assigned to the underworld. All twelve tended to bicker, argue and fall in and out of love with each other, and they would play out their emotions by meddling with the lives of mortals on earth in order to exact revenge on one another.

Through describing these celestial disagreements and emotions, Greek writers were able to give a bigger context to the reasons behind wars, love and natural disasters.

Zeus

Zeus, the lord of the skies, was in charge of the whole clan, and known as the father of the gods. His elevated status seemed to give him licence to sleep with whomever (or whatever) he pleased. And he had a remarkable ability to turn himself into anything he desired in order to get his way, once transforming into a bull to sleep with Europa, who then gave birth to Minos, King of Crete. As a result of such bedroom feats, an extraordinary number of other deities, demigods and beasts claimed Zeus as their father. In fact, at the last count, a progeny of some 120-plus gods and heroes had been attributed to Zeus.

As with many religions, the daddy of them all was

the arbiter of right and wrong. And Zeus seemed a fairly decent fellow when you were on his good side, but he was certainly not someone you'd want to mess with. Zeus is often depicted bearing his trademark thunderbolt, which he'd throw at anyone who had displeased him – something you'd know about if he caught you cheating at poker.

To further complicate matters, Zeus' parents were Cronos and Rhea, and he was married to the very patient Hera (who also happened to be his sister).

The Greek Gods' Family Tree

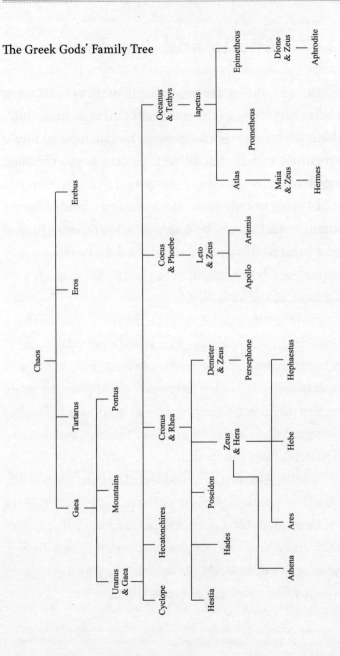

Apollo and Artemis

Apollo was one of the many sons of Zeus, and twin brother of Artemis. In Greek poetry, he represented the sun, with its mysterious passage across the sky being attributed to his chariot pulling it across each day. Conversely, Artemis was represented by the moon. The two of them were born on the hallowed island of Delos, which, to this day, is held sacred, with no one allowed to be born or die on the island. (A far cry from party destination Mykonos, which lies beside Delos and is now in charge of the ancient site.)

Apollo is the god of several things – among them music, truth and healing – as well as being a dab hand at archery. Because of his closeness to Zeus, his astrological importance and his associations with truth, he had many temples dedicated to him – the most famous at Delphi, where the Oracle would channel the god and answer questions about the future.

His sister, Artemis, is the goddess of hunting and wildlife – as well as (contradictorily) childbirth and virginity. There are statues of Artemis from the first and second centuries AD in the ancient city of Ephesus, in what is now Turkey, showing her completely covered in what we assume are bull's testicles, as a sign of her fertility.

Poseidon

Poseidon was often an angry sort. As god of the sea, he was known for stomping his trident to create swells, tsunamis and whirlpools. But if you got him on side, he would happily calm the seas and give you a favourable wind.

He was the brother of Zeus and Hades, and the three of them drew straws for shares of the world after they had overthrown their father, Cronos. Zeus and Poseidon lucked out, gaining control of the land and heavens, and the sea, respectively. Poor Hades drew the short straw and got stuck with the underworld, sometimes referred to as Hades in his honour.

Poseidon happened also to be the father of Polyphemus, the King of the Cyclopes and a one-eyed giant made famous in Homer's *Odyssey* – one of the first myths to be committed to writing in the Western world, and still widely told today. In Homer's epic, the hero Odysseus became trapped in a cave by the one-eyed ogre, but managed to outwit him by plying him with wine. When Polyphemus drunkenly asked Odysseus his name, he replied, 'Nobody,' and drove a burning stake through his one eye. When his fellow Cyclopes were unable to find a person by the name of 'Nobody', Odysseus was left free to sail triumphantly away. But, thinking he was safe at sea, Odysseus mistakenly revealed his name to Polyphemus, who duly ran crying to his father, Poseidon, who in turn banished Odysseus to a few more years lost at sea.

Aphrodite

As the goddess of love, desire and beauty, you would expect everything to be peaceful in the world of Aphrodite, but as the wife of Hephaestus, god of fire, and the lover of Ares, the god of war, hers was a hectic existence.

Her beauty is said to have been the catalyst for the ten-year war of Troy that was central to so many Greek myths: the Trojan Horse, Achilles, Odysseus, Aeneas and the start of the city of Rome, to name just a few (more on that in Chapter 6).

The story goes that, during a banquet held by Zeus, a golden apple inscribed with the words FOR THE MOST BEAUTIFUL WOMAN was thrown into the ceremony by Eris, the goddess of discord. The goddesses Aphrodite, Athena and Hera all claimed the apple for themselves, so it was left to poor mortal Paris, deemed the most eligible bachelor in Troy, to judge who the recipient should be. It wasn't to end well.

The goddesses each undressed and wooed Paris with enticing gifts. But Aphrodite's offer of the hand in marriage of Helen of Troy – the most beautiful mortal in the world – was to prove the most alluring, so Paris gave Aphrodite the golden apple. The trouble was Helen was already married to the Greek king Menelaus, who got a bit annoyed at his wife's infidelities and stormed over to Troy (with hundreds of thousands of Greek soldiers in his wake) to get her back.

Eros

The Greeks had two words for 'love': *agape*, which refers to a kind of deep and soulful love; and *eros*, which refers to more physical desires and needs. It is from this type of love that we get the English word 'erotic'.

Often depicted in Greek art bearing wings and holding his silver bow and arrow, Eros is thought to ignite sexual desire. His perceived personality has changed in art and literature as time has marched on: he appeared as a strapping young man in earlier Greek portrayals and then his character became more mischievous and playful, until Roman (and later) art depicted him as a rotund baby Cupid who flew around firing arrows at gods and mortals to make them fall in love with each other. The iconography of Eros and the arrow through the heart is still widely used today.

Athena

Athena is one of the most revered and likeable goddesses in Greek mythology. Unlike many of her contemporaries, she tended not to act vengefully or to take her anger out on mere mortals. She came to represent the embodiment of all things noble in Greek culture, from wisdom and honesty, to bravery and ferocity in war. She first emerged from Zeus' head (after he had swallowed her pregnant mother, Metis) fully clad in armour and ready for action.

This collection of wonderful traits made Athena the goddess of law and justice, wisdom and courage, and, as such, she acted as a general guardian angel to key characters in both Greek and Roman literature (helping Odysseus and Aeneas out of difficult situations by making them stronger, taller, invisible or disguised, as the scenario required).

The city at the heart of the Greek civilization still bears her name, and her purity as the virgin goddess is celebrated in the Parthenon ('parthenos' means 'virgin' in Greek) that dominates the city's skyline. Both she and Poseidon vied to have the great city dedicated to them. His campaign began first when he struck down his trident to allow seawater to pour from a source in the city; Athena outdid him by planting the first olive tree. Twelve gods presided over the decision and awarded Athena the honour, much to Poseidon's dismay. Depending on which version of the myth you read, Poseidon either did or didn't flood the city with seawater in revenge.

Because of various myths associated with Athena, she is depicted variously in Greek art by her shield, symbols of the olive tree or the wise owl.

Ares

Son of Zeus and Hera, Ares is the personification of war and the brute lust for battle and, while not the only Greek god associated with war, he occupies a specific role within it. For example, Hephaestus concerned himself with the art of creating armour and weaponry, while Athena offered guidance to the Greeks and provided them with a justification for war.

The influence of Ares' wrath features heavily in accounts of war in Greek literature. In one story, Cadmus, the founder of the Greek city Thebes, and his band of men went in search of Cadmus' sister Europa, who had been abducted by Zeus. Advised to follow the first cow they came across, Cadmus and his tribe set off on their trip. They soon encountered a spring that was guarded by a snake (who, rather worryingly, happened to be the offspring of Ares), which then killed Cadmus' band of men. In retaliation, Cadmus killed the snake with a rock.

Athena advised Cadmus to remove some of the snake's teeth and bury them in the soil, and from this an army of men – known as the Spartoi – emerged and helped Cadmus to found the city of Thebes. Unfortunately for Cadmus, Ares wrecked his revenge for the slaying of the snake by forcing him to work as his slave for an entire year. Although Cadmus went on to take Ares' daughter, Harmonia, as his wife, the two of them were turned later into snakes themselves.

Hades

Ruler of the underworld, Hades is, not unsurprisingly, perceived as an angry sort. His name is also used to refer to the underworld itself, and it is here that everyone is consigned to after death. Rather than the heaven and hell of Christianity, the Greeks had just one place for the dead, although there are many different places within Hades, some of which are far more desirable than others.

According to Greek mythology, very few managed to enter Hades and return to earth alive, which is not surprising given the difficult journey it entailed. It began with an excursion by ferry across the black river Acheron, with the deity Charon acting as oarsman. His services didn't come cheap, and it is for this reason that the Greeks – and the Romans – placed a coin in the mouth of the dear departed before they were cremated.

On the other side of the Acheron, the situation

deteriorated further. The huge and violent three-headed dog Cerberus (a figure that has cropped up in literature ever since, and even had a cameo in the first *Harry Potter* book) guarded the passage to the region of Erebus, where lay the river Lethe – from which the dead souls drank in order to forget their earthly lives. In front of the palace of Hades, all entrants' lives were judged, and the outcome of this decision determined where they would spend eternity. Tartarus was the home of horrendous punishment, while in the fields of Elysium (which gave their name to one of the most prominent roads in Paris, the Champs-Élysées) one could reside joyfully among the grass and flowers.

Hephaestus

Hephaestus is the god of fire, volcanoes, metalwork and sculpture and he can be recognized in Greek art by the hammer and tongs he carries and by his penchant for riding a donkey. It was the highest honour to receive a set of armour made by him personally, as Achilles did before he went into battle in Homer's *Iliad*. Hephaestus also created the armoury for the remaining gods on Mount Olympus.

In contrast to the skill and intricate nature of his handiwork, Hephaestus is known as a lame god. Reports vary, but we do know that he had a slightly deformed leg following a fall from the top of Mount Olympus.

Other stories suggest his leg was withered from birth, and his mother, Hera, disgusted at her son's deformity, flung him down to earth. There, Hephaestus landed in the sea and was retrieved, rather fortunately, and raised by Eurynome and Thetis (mother of Achilles) on the volcanic island of Lemnos – where he honed his skill as a master craftsman.

Another version of the myth sees Hephaestus acquiring his leg injury after being flung from the peak of Mount Olympus as a fully grown god, which resulted in his leg injury. According to this legend, Zeus was angry at his wife, Hera, for setting a storm on Heracles as he returned from Troy, and so, as punishment, Zeus hung Hera in chains from Olympus. When Hephaestus went to his mother's rescue, Zeus grabbed him by the leg and flung him down the mountain. His fall lasted for an entire day, ending on the island of Lemnos, just as the sun was setting.

Cronos

Although Zeus is the father of the gods, he was the son of Cronos, who himself was the offspring of Gaia (the earth) and Uranus (the sky). Cronos married his sister Rhea and together they produced the gods and goddesses of Mount Olympus, including, in addition to Zeus, Hera (who also became Zeus' wife), Hades and Poseidon, among others.

Cronos took over power of the heavens from his father Uranus by castrating him with a jagged-toothed sickle. After a prophecy revealed he too would face the same fate at the hands of his own sons, Cronos took matters into his own hands by swallowing each child that Rhea produced. Only the youngest son, Zeus, avoided this same fate when Rhea managed to give birth to him in secret in a mountain cave in Crete. To deceive her husband, Rhea gave him a rock covered up in a blanket under the pretence it was their son, which Cronos quickly devoured in one gulp.

Once Zeus came of age, he liberated his grown siblings from Cronos' belly. And, following a vicious ten-year war against his father's generation of Greek gods, the Titans, Zeus was victorious, and Cronos and his fellow Titans were driven down into Tartarus in the underworld. The way was paved for the next generation of gods: the Olympians.

Gaia

As the goddess of earth and the mother of all, Gaia is the Greek gods' matriarchal figure. It was from her unions with Uranus (the sky), Pontus (the sea) and Tartarus (the underworld) that all other gods were created. There are elements of the 'earth mother' figure in many other belief systems, and it is thought her existence in Greek culture is a mythological hangover from an earlier time.

Despite her motherly role, Gaia was not averse to trouble. It was she who helped her son Cronos overthrow and castrate Uranus. And when she had tired of Cronos' antics she assisted her grandson Zeus in his overthrow of the Titans to become leader of the gods. Her work did not stop there. Angry that Zeus had committed Cronos to the underworld, Gaia enlisted the help of the Gigantes and the monster Typhoeus to dispatch Zeus, too. However, her grandson was too great a match.

The Muses

In Greek mythology, the Titan goddess Mnemosyne was the personification of memory (her name deriving from the Greek word for 'mindful', and which is perpetuated in English words such as 'mnemonic'). She was also the mother of the Muses, the nine sisters who inspired all the arts, following a nine-day romance with Zeus.

MUSE	AREA OF INSPIRATION	OFTEN SEEN CARRYING
Calliope	Muse of Epic Poetry	a writing tablet
Clio	Muse of History	scrolls
Erato	Muse of Lyric Poetry	a cithara (an instrument of the lyre family)
Euterpe	Muse of Music	a flute-like instrument
Melpomene	Muse of Tragedy	a tragic mask
Polyhymnia	Muse of Hymns	a veil
Terpsichore	Muse of Light Verse and Dance	a lyre
Thalia	Muse of Comedy	a comic mask
Urania	Muse of Astronomy	a globe or compass

Many of the great works of Greek – and Roman – literature open with an invocation to the Muses to inspire the poet in his or her telling of a particular myth. The concept of writers and artists – and others, such as astronomers – being inspired by Muses continued in Western art and literature for many centuries, as in the Prologue to Act I of Shakespeare's *King Henry V*, which begins, 'O! for a Muse of fire, that would ascend / The brightest heaven of invention.'

Even today, fashion designers speak of having a 'muse' in one particular model or celebrity, whose body shape, personality or style they will use as inspiration in their development of new designs.

Adonis

Yet another Greek god associated with the enduring theme of love and desire, Adonis, the god of plants and rebirth, was a beautiful man who, even as a youngster, was able to attract the attentions of the goddess of love, Aphrodite. With the young Adonis under her charge, Aphrodite gave him to Persephone, goddess of spring and queen of the underworld (see below), to look after in her absence.

Persephone, too, became enamoured with Adonis and was reluctant to return him to Aphrodite when the time came. A dispute ensued, settled only by Zeus' decree that Adonis split his time equally between Aphrodite, Persephone and a destination of his choosing. Unfortunately for Persephone, Adonis made his allegiances clear when he chose to spend his free time with Aphrodite – a union that so angered Aphrodite's lover Ares that he disguised himself as a wild boar and killed Adonis in a jealous rage. He died in Aphrodite's arms.

Persephone

A rather sad character, Persephone is the goddess of spring and the daughter of Zeus and Demeter, and her story is used to explain the changing of the seasons. Although Persephone's mother tried hard to shield her daughter from the many amorous celestial suitors, her efforts were thwarted when one afternoon while Persephone was happily picking flowers in a field, Hades, god of the underworld, appeared and abducted Persephone and took her as his wife.

Angry at this violation, Demeter demanded Hades return her daughter. Hades eventually relented, but, by this stage, Persephone had tasted her husband's delicious pomegranate fruits, and, as such, was bound to return there as his wife and queen of the underworld for half the year. In her absence, the mortal world was plunged into winter and spring only reappeared when she returned bi-annually to ground level.

Dione

Zeus is thought to have sired children with up to approximately sixty different goddesses and women, one of whom was Dione. Her name, quite simply, is a female version of 'Zeus' – derived from the same root from which we get the words 'divine', 'deity', 'Diana' and 'Jupiter'. She is the mother of Aphrodite – who herself is one of the very ancient goddesses – and, as such, Dione's appearance in Greek mythology is similar to that of earth mother Gaia.

Dione's appearances in ancient texts are fleeting, but in the few words attributed to her she exposes a rarely seen aspect of the Greek gods' vulnerability. After her daughter, Aphrodite, was wounded in the War of Troy while trying to protect her own son, Aeneas (more on him on page 176), she returned to her mother on Mount Olympus for comfort. As Dione took care of Aphrodite, she reminded her that immortals too have their weaknesses. To illustrate her point, she told Aphrodite of an incident when the war god Ares was once held prisoner inside a cauldron by two brutish brother giants, and it was only after the intervention of the giants' stepmother, who enlisted the help of Hermes, that the war god was rescued. Dione also tells how the great gods Hera and Hades were once injured by Heracles' weapons.

HEROES, HEROINES, VILLAINS AND MONSTERS

Y ou will find you are familiar with many of these heroes of Greek mythology.

Heracles (Hercules)

Heracles is known more widely by his Roman name, Hercules, and was respected for his size and strength, his quick wit and his skill as a fighter. He made the transition from mythical warrior hero to the status of immortal god, and was worshipped as such later on. He was the son of Zeus and the mortal Alcmene (after Zeus disguised himself as her husband), and it is said that Zeus' wife, Hera, focused her energies on hating and being jealous of Heracles for this reason.

Driven mad by Hera, Heracles murdered his children.

To atone for his behaviour, he was required to carry out twelve near-impossible heroic tasks devised by his nemesis, Eurystheus, who had deposed him as king. The completion of these tasks would cleanse Heracles' soul and propel him into immortality.

These myths originate from the Greeks' interest in astrology: it is thought that each of the twelve labours once referred to an animal seen in the night-time constellations – some of which are still familiar today. For more on our modern-day constellations and the myths associated with them see pages 174–84.

THE TWELVE LABOURS OF HERACLES

1. Kill the Nemean Lion

A huge creature was wreaking havoc in Nemea: a lion whose hide was thought to be impenetrable. Heracles' first task was to kill it. Heracles was able to corner the beast and wrestle it to the ground, whereupon he took its pelt (and he is often depicted in Greek art and sculpture wearing the hide). Hera immortalized the lion in the constellation Leo.

2. Slay the Lernaean Hydra

The Hydra was a nine-headed sea snake, which Heracles was sent to destroy. But each time he cut off one of its heads, two more would grow in its place, making the task insurmountable. To make matters worse, the Hydra was assisted by a giant crab, which further impeded Heracles' efforts. Not to be outsmarted, with the help of his nephew, Iolaus, Heracles set a burning torch onto the severed necks of the Hydra, preventing further heads from growing. He also killed the crab by squashing it underfoot. Both beasts were then placed into the stars by Hera as the Hydra and Cancer constellations.

3. Capture the Cerynitian Hind

The next task was to retrieve the Cerynitian Hind, a golden-horned deer sacred to the goddess Artemis. After chasing the animal for an entire year, Heracles finally managed to get hold of it, but only after a significant struggle during which one of the animal's sacred horns came unstuck. Despite her annoyance at this minor destruction, Artemis allowed Heracles to borrow the animal for his remaining quests.

4. Capture the Erymanthean Boar

Heracles pursued this huge beast around the snowy sides of Mount Erymanthos, until he was able to capture it in a net and bring it back to Eurystheus – who was so startled by the creature that he jumped into a huge jar to hide.

5. Clean the Augean Stables

King Augeas of Elis kept a huge herd of 1,000 cattle, and Heracles' task was to clean out the stables, which had not been undertaken in several decades. Heracles set about his task by diverting nearby rivers to flow through the stables. After Augeas failed to honour his promise to give 100 of the cattle to Heracles if he completed the task in one day, Heracles launched an attack on Elis. When he was eventually victorious, it is said that he started the first Olympic Games in celebration.

6. Kill the Stymphalian Birds

These man-eating beasts terrorized Lake Stymphalis in Arcadia. Heracles was able to kill them one by one with his bow and arrow, having first startled them into the air by using a rattle. It is thought they are represented by the constellations Aquila (eagle) and Cygnus (swan), which lie in the night sky either side of Sagitta (representing Heracles' arrow).

7. Capture the Cretan Bull

This huge white bull was sent to Crete from the sea by Poseidon, where it seduced King Minos' wife, Pasiphaë. She even had a fake wooden cow created in which she could submerge herself to fulfil her desires, after which she mothered the half-man half-beast Minotaur (see page 163, and the story of Europa [page 165] for a similar tale). Heracles was, of course, successful in his attempt to capture the bull, which is remembered as the Taurus constellation.

8. Steal the Mares of Diomedes

Next in Heracles' list of tasks was to steal the horses of the violent King Diomedes. Heracles took with him a few young companions to help, including his favoured companion Abderus, whose job it was to look after the horses while Heracles and the others attended to Diomedes. Unfortunately, Heracles and his men were unaware that the horses were ferocious, flesh-eating maniacs, and so when they returned they found Abderus had been killed. Heracles held the lifeless body in his arms and wept. He then created a tomb for the boy, upon which site the city of Abdera was founded many years later. After binding the horses' mouths shut, Heracles and his remaining companions were able to return them to King Eurystheus.

9. Get the Girdle of Hippolyta

Hippolyta was queen of the Amazons – a group of brutal female warriors – and she was the proud owner of a belt made by Ares, the god of war. Although Hippolyta was quite willing to hand over the belt to Heracles, which Eurystheus' daughter had her keen eye on, Hera started a rumour among the Amazons that Heracles was there to steal the queen herself. Chaos ensued. After the Amazons attacked Heracles, he retaliated by killing Hippolyta and stealing the belt.

10. Steal the Cattle of Geryon

A three-headed, three-bodied monster, Geryon resided on the island of Erytheia, where he kept a herd of cows that had been coloured red by the setting sun of the west. Heracles travelled to the island in a golden cup-boat given to him by Helios, the sun god, whereupon he set about his task. Heracles first killed the cattle-herder Eurytion, followed by the two-headed guard dog Orthrus, and used a bow dipped in the blood of the Hydra (see page 153) to kill Geryon. He faced a bit of a task in returning the cattle to Eurystheus – not helped by Hera placing a gadfly in the herd to disrupt and disperse them – but he succeeded in the end.

But Heracles then faced further struggle: although Eurystheus had initially told him that he had just ten tasks to complete, he decided to add two more – on the basis that Heracles had received help with killing the Hydra, and had received payment in cows in the Augean stables. Undeterred, Heracles pressed on.

11. Steal the Apples of the Hesperides

The Hesperides were three goddesses who looked after a tree of golden apples and their story relates to the setting sun. ('Hesperos' in Greek means 'evening', and the word is associated with anything to do with the golden sunset and the west.) The story of Heracles' triumph varies according to which version you read. One story suggests Heracles slew the hundred-headed serpent that guarded the tree before making off with a punnet of apples. Another myth tells how he offered to hold up the whole world for Atlas in exchange for his collecting the apples (in this version, Atlas is related to the Hesperides, which means he already has them onside). When Atlas returned with the apples, he seemed happy for Heracles to continue holding up the world. Surprisingly, Heracles agreed, but on one condition: Atlas had to relieve him temporarily so he could adjust his cloak to make it more comfortable . . . at which point Heracles made an inevitable dash, golden apples in hand.

12. Fetch Cerberus

Of all the labours of Heracles, this was undoubtedly the toughest. Cerberus was the vicious three-headed guard dog in the underworld (see more on Hades on page 141), and certainly not the sort of beast you'd happily take out on a leash. Cerberus was the sibling of the Hydra as well as of Orthrus, the two-headed guard dog of Geryon's cattle. He was also the uncle to the Nemean Lion.

As the first mortal to attempt a round trip to Hades, Heracles first visited a priest who conducted rituals by invoking the myth of Persephone (see page 149). Heracles climbed down into the underworld, eventually overpowering Cerberus with his bare hands and bringing him up to Eurystheus. Unlike many of Heracles' other conquests, Cerberus was later returned to Hades unharmed.

Perseus and Medusa

King Acrisius of Argos was once told by an oracle that he would be killed by the son of his daughter, Danae, which led the king to lock her away from the prying eyes of the world's suitors. Despite this intervention, Zeus came in disguise as a golden shower and impregnated Danae. When she gave birth to her son, Perseus, the two were cast off to sea by Acrisius, landing on the island of Seriphus.

As a grown man, Perseus was commanded by King Polydectes to bring back the head of Medusa – the fearsome beast with serpents lashing out of her head. One look at her would turn you to stone (the literal meaning of the word 'petrify'), but such warnings did not stop Perseus. With the help of the goddess Athena, Perseus hatched a plan of attack, equipped with Athena's mirrored shield. His journey saw him visiting the Graiai – three old, haggard, witch-like sisters who shared one eye and one tooth, and who have appeared across literature and film, such as in Shakespeare's *Macbeth* and any number of witch-related movies (*Hocus Pocus*, *The Witches of Eastwick* and *Stardust* to name just three).

Eventually, Perseus reached Medusa and, using the mirrored shield to direct his weapons, was able to kill her and remove her head without looking at her and risking petrifaction. He returned to Seriphus and revealed the head to King Polydectes, which immediately turned the king to stone.

Perseus returned to his homeland and successfully overthrew his grandfather, who flees. Much later, the oracle's prophecy is finally realized when at a ceremonial games Perseus' errant discus kills his grandfather.

Midas

The origin of this well-known tale was used by the Greeks to explain the presence of gold in the Pactolus river on what is now the Turkish coast of the Aegean Sea. Following a favour, King Midas was granted one wish by the god Dionysus. Without a moment's pause, the king wished that everything he touched turned to gold.

For a while, life was wonderful: Midas freely indulged his new found powers, turning his chariots, livestock and his garden into useless – but valuable – lumps of gleaming gold. But this joy was short-lived, however, as King Midas soon realized the difficulties of having every item of food and drink turned to glistening metal. Events took a turn for the worse when, having taken his daughter by the hand to demonstrate his new party trick, his horror was complete: she turned to gold. Thankfully, Dionysus listened to Midas' disgusted regret and allowed him to wash away his new skill in the Pactolus river, after which all of his possessions, including his daughter, were returned to their original state.

'The Midas touch' is a phrase often attributed now to successful businesspeople in a complimentary manner. Rather alarmingly, we use it only to refer to positive short-term gain and we seem to have forgotten that Midas nearly starved to death, temporarily killed his daughter and immediately regretted his power.

Croesus

A wonderful offshoot of Midas' dalliance with alchemy is that the gold in the Pactolus river went on to make another man very rich indeed. The stories of Croesus blur happily between fact and myth; we know that he was indeed the last King of Lydia, ruling over much of modern-day Turkey in the sixth century BC. But because of his colossal wealth he soon became a character of legend, which became more fantastical as time went on – and within a few centuries the myths around him were no longer necessarily placed in the right chronology.

One story involving the king tells how he was visited by travelling Athenian Solon. Croesus showed off all of his wonderful possessions and riches, and asked whether Solon knew of anyone who could be more blessed than he. Not being a man of tact, Solon answered that he knew of three others who were more blessed than Croesus – mere commoners who had passed their lives in brave and noble ways, and who had all died having lived a good life, despite having no riches. Solon told the king it was only after someone had died that you could look back to see whether or not they should be thought of as the most blessed person.

And the real King Croesus did indeed become a touch too sure of himself when he decided in 547 BC to launch a pre-emptive strike against the Persians, who seemed to be on a path of growth. Upon seeking advice from several oracles before the attack, Croesus was told that if he were to fight the Persians it would result in the destruction of a great empire. Sadly for Croesus, it was his own empire that he would destroy.

Theseus and
the Minotaur

Another mythical hero who came to embody all things Greek, manly and brave, Theseus was the son of King Aegeus of Athens and the sea god Poseidon, both having copulated with Aethra. His dual paternity bestowed upon him a prince-like stature as well as lending him a touch of the divine, which enabled him to call upon the gods for help when needed.

Greece as we know it today didn't exist as one entity, and instead was a collection of many different city-states, each with its own king, but nonetheless unified through similar languages centred on Athens. In Crete, King Minos was a fearful ruler, and, following an altercation with Athens, he demanded that seven young men and seven young women should each year board a black-sailed ship to Crete to be sacrificed to the Minotaur. Half-man and half-bull, the beast was the result of a union between a bull and either Europa or Pasiphaë (according to which myth you read), and it lived hidden away in King Minos' inescapable labyrinth.

Theseus endeavoured to put an end to this tradition and become a hero among his people, and so he volunteered himself as one of the seven young men. When in Minos' palace in Knossos, Theseus was visited by the king's daughter Ariadne. She gave him a ball of silk thread and told him to unwind it as he travelled through the labyrinth to help him find his way out. Theseus did as she suggested and bravely killed the Minotaur. Upon leaving the palace triumphantly, Theseus decided to take Ariadne home with him, but his attempts were thwarted by the god Dionysus, who instructed him to leave her on the island of Naxos since the god wanted her for his own bride.

In his grief, Theseus returned to Athens and forgot to change the sails of the ship from black to white. King Aegeus saw the ship approaching from a distance and feared the worst. Without waiting to confirm his concerns, he hurled himself into the sea that now bears his name.

Theseus then became king of Athens, and unified the Attic states into one notional country. Since this unification actually took place over a number of centuries, we can assume the myth of Theseus to be an allegory of the 'Greekness' he embodied. Minos was known for his barbaric and draconian punishments, so it is easy to see how a foreign king in a huge sprawling palace could be muddled into a mythical beast living in a confusing labyrinth (of which there is no evidence in Knossos). In slaying the barbaric non-Greek monster and overcoming the Cretan king, the hero Theseus acts as a perfectly virile personification of the Greek people.

Europa

Europa's name has been bestowed not only on one of the moons of Jupiter (the planet) but also on the continent of Europe. She was by all accounts a very pretty young girl of the nobility – so pretty, in fact, that Zeus felt the urge to disguise himself as a docile white bull in order to seduce her.

Europa approached the seemingly unthreatening animal and began to caress it and decorate it with flowers. Eventually, she decided to climb upon its back, at which point Zeus ran at full speed into the sea and swam all the way to Crete, with the girl still mounted on top.

A procession of nymphs, spirits and other gods joined them on their journey and encouraged Europa to consider that this was no ordinary white bull; she quickly cottoned on to the idea that he might be a god.

By Zeus, she bore three sons, including King Minos of Crete, who was famous for his brutality and possession of the mythical Minotaur (see above). Europa was also the sister of Cadmus, who, during his search for his abducted sister, had incurred the wrath of Ares, as seen earlier in this chapter (on page 140).

Icarus

The story of Icarus and his craftsman father, Daedalus, is a moral one, acting as a heartbreaking way to warn us of the importance of humility. There are similarities between this myth and the Chinese Kua Fu (see page 72), showing the way in which different civilizations have devised similar allegorical tales to demonstrate universal life lessons.

According to Greek mythology, Icarus and Daedalus were held captive inside King Minos' great labyrinth in Crete, which Daedalus had built for the king. Daedalus had been the one to give Minos' daughter, Ariadne, the ball of string that helped Theseus find his way out of the labyrinth (see page 164). Despite not knowing the way out of his own construction, Daedalus is said to have had great ingenuity, and skilfully cobbled together two sets of wings from feathers held together with wax for him and his son to make their escape away from Crete.

Daedalus warned his son not to fly too close to the sun, to follow him closely and avoid making his own path. Needless to say, Icarus failed to heed his father's advice and flew higher and higher in the sky. But the closer he got to the sun, the warmer the wax became, until he could flap no more and he plunged into the sea. There exists today an island called Ikaria, which is sited in an area of the Aegean Sea known as the Ikarian Sea – the place at which Icarus is said to have fallen so many years ago.

CHAPTER 8:

ROMAN MYTHOLOGY

WHO WERE THE ROMANS?

More than any other civilization, the Romans can lay claim to having had the biggest impact on modern Western society. And yet, much of what they introduced had, in fact, been acquired from Greece – from the gods of Greek mythology, to its law, art, philosophy, literature, society, theatre and technology.

Roman civilization lasted for more than a thousand years, encompassing at its height much of western and northern Europe, North Africa and the Middle East. What began as a group of settlements joined together to form the city of Rome by 600 BC. In 509 BC, it became a republic, ruled by two consuls elected from the senate, and, growing in strength, Rome soon overpowered the other settlers on the Italian peninsula.

By 146 BC, Rome had acquired her first overseas territories – Sicily, Spain and North Africa – and the Macedonian wars that followed saw further acquisitions in Macedonia, Greece and Asia Minor. In 27 BC, Julius Caesar's son became the first emperor of Rome and imperial rule was to continue for the next 400 years.

By the second century AD, the Roman Empire covered all of the Mediterranean, most of western and southern Europe and even extended across what is modern-day Turkey, Israel, Egypt, Iraq, Iran and parts of Saudi Arabia. However, in its dying days, the empire's sheer size made it vulnerable to attack from northern Europe. By AD 455, Germanic tribes had sacked Rome itself and, in AD 476, the last Roman Emperor, Romulus Augustus, abdicated, signalling the collapse of the empire.

Gods and Goddesses

The Romans were so enamoured with Greek mythology they adopted its pantheon of gods and goddesses and their accompanying stories. In fact, much of what we know about Greek mythology actually comes from Latin literature. As such, rather than recount the myths already told in Chapter 7 below is a conversion table of the Greek and Latin names. You will notice that the planets in our solar system have all been named after the top Roman gods (with the exception of Earth).

GREEK NAME	LATIN EQUIVALENT	WHO'S WHO
Aphrodite	Venus	Goddess of love and beauty
Apollo	Apollo	God of music, the sun, archery
Ares	Mars	God of war
Artemis	Diana	Goddess of hunting, fertility
Athena	Minerva	Goddess of wisdom, courage, protection
Cronos	Saturn	God of the sky, ruler of the Titans
Demeter	Ceres	Goddess of agriculture (cf. English 'cereal')
Dionysus	Bacchus	God of wine
Eros	Cupid	God of love and desire
Hades	Pluto	God of the underworld
Hephaestus	Vulcan	God of fire, volcanoes, weaponry
Hera	Juno	Wife of Zeus / Jupiter
Heracles	Hercules	General manly hero and demigod
Hermes	Mercury	Messenger of the gods, with winged sandals
Persephone	Proserpina	Wife of Hades / Pluto
Poseidon	Neptune	God of the sea
Uranus	Uranus	The sky, father of the Titans
Zeus	Jupiter	Ruler of the gods, adept with a lightning bolt

THE ORIGINS OF ROME: PICK A STORY

S tories differ regarding the beginnings of the great city of Rome, which was the beating heart of the Romans' colossal empire that ruled the Mediterranean for 2,000 years. The earlier myths tend to use the story of the twins Romulus and Remus, who were brought up by a wolf, to describe the founding of the city of Rome, but later myths, such as Virgil's poem about Aeneas, depict a Trojan hero descended directly from the gods as the city's noble founder. (Virgil manages to insert Romulus and Remus as a footnote into his story, so as not to disquiet the traditionalists.)

Romulus and Remus

Most of us might be able to recall the story of the twins brought up by a wolf, but perhaps not how (or why) the myth was chosen to depict the origins of Rome. After the twin brothers were deserted by their father, Mars, the god of war, they were brought up in the woods by a wolf (an icon of fear).

But their new-found stability was not to last long because, in 753 BC, Romulus killed his brother during an argument and founded a city to celebrate, to which he gave his own name. In an effort to populate his newly established city, Romulus began to steal women against their will from the nearby region of Sabinum – a scene captured in countless pieces of Renaissance art as the Rape of the Sabine Women.

It seems strange that such a proud civilization came from such inauspicious beginnings, but perhaps it is this sense of arrogant pride that made the Romans so successful: their feeling of superiority allowed them to expand the empire with great strength. And, with such a bold myth as their starting point, the Romans perhaps gave the population a sense of entitlement that worked in the empire's favour.

Aeneas

In 29 BC, Augustus Caesar, the first official emperor of the Roman Empire, commissioned Virgil to write an epic poem about the founding of Rome. The empire had been the victim of years of external strife and civil war, following a series of dictatorships that led to the collapse of the Roman Republic and its rebirth as the empire. Augustus Caesar wanted a piece of literature to instil a sense of pride in Rome and cement his precarious position by telling the story of the city's beginnings. The poem also conveniently links Augustus and his family by heritage to the very founders of the city, never mind that he was actually adopted by Julius Caesar.

In *The Aeneid*, Virgil tells of the Trojan hero Aeneas as he travelled away from defeat by the Greeks in the ten-year War of Troy to find a new home in Italy. The legend borrows unapologetically from the two great works of Greek poet Homer, *The Iliad* and *The Odyssey* (deemed to be the first compositions ever committed to writing in the Western world). Virgil uses the Greek myths that Roman citizens would have grown up with and makes them uniquely and boldly Roman – aligning the new Roman Empire with the very ancient stories told over many generations around the Mediterranean.

The most moving tale within *The Aeneid* is that of Aeneas and Dido. She is the Queen of Carthage who falls in love with Aeneas on his journey to Italy. Venus (goddess of love, and also Aeneas' mother) encourages this burgeoning romance by conjuring up a storm, which sees the two seek shelter together in a cave.

But ultimately, Aeneas is reminded by Jupiter's messenger, Mercury, that his duty is to found Rome, and that he must leave behind his love and carnal urges for Dido if he is to fulfil his fate. Aeneas explains to Dido that he must go, and his ships set sail. In her pain, the queen wisely prophesies an everlasting conflict between Carthage and the future Rome, and then kills herself using a sword Aeneas had given her.

The light from her burning pyre is seen by Aeneas as his fleet sails away, and he knows then what she has done. *The Aeneid*'s emotive passages about Dido's heartache and subsequent suicide make this one of the great love stories of Western literature. Aeneas later meets his former flame in the underworld and tries to explain his actions, but her ghost remains chillingly silent, refusing to look him in the eyes.

THE SIGNS OF THE ZODIAC

The signs of the zodiac are a wonderful example of how myths can spread from one civilization to another. The term 'zodiac' originally comes from a Greek phrase meaning a 'circle of animals', which refers to the circular astrological chart that is split into twelve sections, each with its own representation of a different animal. But this concept predates the Greeks even, seen nearly 3,000 years ago with the Sumerians and Babylonians (in modern-day Iraq). Even some of the same animal characters were used in those earliest versions.

Every civilization has looked to the stars in wonder, and humans have created many wonderful stories for the shapes we see in them and in their movement across the sky. It is through this stargazing that we have developed as navigators both on our own planet and beyond it.

The Greeks had their own interpretations of the constellations, some of which are included here, and some of which have their own origin myths from the Labours of Heracles (see page 152). The Romans adopted and subsequently Romanized the names, and several thousand years later they are still showing their influence in newspaper horoscopes the world over. The Babylonians would be pleased.

Latin name (used in English)	English translation	Why?
Aries	Ram	There have been many goat-related myths across the world, but the Greeks and Romans settled on the golden-fleeced ram, the coat of which Jason and his Argonauts were tasked with stealing from King Aeetes of Colchis.
Taurus	Bull	This constellation is believed to have been identified as looking like a bull from as staggeringly far back as 15,000 BC. The Greek and Roman myth of the constellation was about either Jupiter disguised as a bull to seduce Europa, or about Heracles' capture of the Cretan Bull (see page 155).

Latin name (used in English)	English translation	Why?
Gemini	Twins	The twins Castor and Pollux can be seen as stick men drawn into the stars. They are brothers of Helen of Troy (whose abduction started the great War of Troy) and Clytemnestra (who murdered her husband Agamemnon after the war). The two boys are associated with horsemanship and navigation. Pollux and Helen emerged from one egg after Zeus disguised himself as a swan to rape their mother, Leda, and from another egg emerged Castor and Clytemnestra, fathered by Tyndareus. Therefore, only Pollux was immortal, but Zeus granted his brother immortality in the stars.
Cancer	Crab	The crab has a rather uninspiring role to play in classical mythology, appearing as a snapping accomplice to the Lernaean Hydra that Hercules must defeat (see page 153). Hercules dispatches the beast by squishing it underfoot – and now it resides in the stars.
Leo	Lion	The lion is another shape recognized very early on – by the Mesopotamians as early as 4000 BC. The Greeks and Romans associate it with the myth of Hercules overcoming the Nemean Lion (see page 152).

Latin name (used in English)	English translation	Why?
Virgo	Virgin	This constellation shows a female figure in the night sky. As such, she has been associated with a variety of characters. Earlier Babylonians associated these stars with agricultural fertility, and that remains with the Romans, who associate the female form with Ceres (goddess of agriculture) and depicted her carrying a frond. Other myths name the constellation as Justitia (goddess of justice), with her close proximity to the scales of justice in neighbouring constellation Libra.
Libra	Scales	The stars that make up the scales in the sky used to be the claws of the Greek Scorpio constellation, but the Romans turned the claws into its own distinct constellation of balancing scales. (A little creative licence is needed when observing shapes in the stars.) The aspect of Earth against the stars changes over time, so Libra used to be visible in the sky during the autumn equinox – with the equal balance of night and day fitting well with this imagery. In the modern day, we are in Virgo when we reach this equinox.

Latin name (used in English)	English translation	Why?
Scorpio	Scorpion	The scorpion, whether dismembered by the Romans or not, lies close to the constellation of Orion and it rises in the night sky just as the stars of Orion set on the horizon. As such, the scorpion is seen as an adversary from which he is running away – either sent by Diana in retaliation for Orion's unwanted advances, or sent by the Earth in response to his boast that he could slay any beast.
Sagittarius	Archer	This constellation depicts a centaur – the torso of a man and the body and legs of a horse – aiming his bow and arrow at the neighbouring scorpion.
Capricorn	Horned goat/fish	This half-goat half-fish figure appears on the winter solstice on 21 December. As such, he represented the start of winter for many millennia before the Greeks or Romans adopted the association. They called him Pan (Greek) or Faunus (Roman), and the myth goes that he was hiding from the monster Typhon, who was sent to fight the gods. He dipped into the Nile and changed his bottom half to that of a fish to help his escape. Jupiter immortalized him in the stars as gratitude for various good deeds he had done for the gods.

Latin name (used in English)	English translation	Why?
Aquarius	Water-bearer	With one of the most ambitious interpretations, this constellation depicts a young man pouring water from an amphora jug. In classical mythology, he is associated with a young boy called Ganymede (Greek) or Catamitus (the Latin transliteration). Zeus was enamoured with him and so disguised himself as an eagle to abduct the boy and take him to Mount Olympus, where he became the gods' cup-bearer. This story is depicted by the nearby constellation of Aquila (Latin for 'eagle').
Pisces	Fish	The two fish depicted here joined by a cord are said to represent Venus and her son Cupid as they escaped the terrible monster Typhon, who was sent to kill the gods. While Faunus (the Capricorn) went for a dip in the Nile to escape, this pair transformed themselves entirely into fish.

The Gemini Constellation

The Leo Constellation

Heroes and Heroines

These Roman tales owe much to Greek mythology.

Orpheus and Eurydice

This tragic love story is told most beautifully by Ovid in his poetry compilation *Metamorphoses*, in which he provides a host of myths to explain everything from the origins of the butterfly to the laurel tree.

Orpheus and Eurydice were very much in love, but soon after they were married she was bitten by a snake and died. Orpheus was overwhelmed with grief and felt he had nothing to live for other than the mesmerizing song of his lyre. Orpheus made the bold journey into Hades (or Aides, as the Romans called it) and implored Pluto and Proserpina with his entrancing music to return his wife to the realm of the living. His music was so staggeringly beautiful that the whole of the underworld stopped for a moment.

They were so moved that Proserpina could not refuse – on one condition: that Orpheus lead his wife all the way up to the mortal world without looking at her once, and only set eyes on her once they had arrived. Together, the reunited pair made the long climb up the steep and dark path, with Eurydice limping behind.

As they neared the entrance to Hades, the darkness gradually faded and Orpheus was so desperate to make sure his wife made it over the threshold that he looked back. He knew immediately it was too soon, and straight away Eurydice sank back into the underworld muttering a faint 'farewell' to her former flame. Orpheus reached out to touch her three times, but three times his hands went through nothingness where she had once stood.

Orpheus had lost his wife twice and was not allowed to re-enter the underworld. With nothing left to live for, he traipsed about with his lyre waiting for his fate, which arrived in the form of a group of female spirits called the Maenades. They set about tearing poor Orpheus limb from limb, after which they created a shrine for him at the base of Mount Olympus. Even now, the song of the nightingales at this site is said to be the most beautiful in the world.

The Trojan Horse

Another distinctly Greek tale that is retold in more detail in Virgil's *Aeneid* (more on that previously on page 176).

The story of the Trojan Horse takes place towards the end of the ten-year War of Troy, in which the Greeks tried to retrieve Helen, daughter of Zeus and the wife of King Menelaus of Sparta in Greece, who had been gifted to Paris of Troy by the goddess Venus. The war had been raging for almost a decade but the walled city of Troy looked to remain fighting fit.

A cunning plan was hatched by the Greeks: they retreated in their hundreds of ships until they were just out of sight, which is where they hid in an attempt to convince the Trojans they had surrendered. As a gift to the supposed victors, the Greeks left a huge wooden horse outside the city walls. The Trojans duly accepted the gift and hauled it into the city.

Unfortunately for the Romans, this was no generous offering, for inside the structure were some forty Greek men, led by the heroic Odysseus of Homer's great poem. This band of soldiers emerged from the horse in the dead of night to be joined by their allies, who had come out of hiding. Together they caused mass devastation in the city, leading to a Greek victory and the fall of Troy.

Manlius and the Geese of Rome

The Roman historian Livy tells us the story of how Rome was saved by an excitable gaggle of geese. In about 390 BC, the Gauls staged an attack on the Roman troops outside the city. Many soldiers lost their lives, some even jumping into the River Tiber and drowning through the weight of their armour. The survivors retreated to the Capitoline Hill, with women and children taken safely out to the outlying city districts, while the Gauls laid siege.

Despite food becoming a treasured commodity for those marooned on the hill, some still gave a small portion of what they had to the flock of geese that lived there with them, since they were sacred to Juno, the wife of Jupiter. This generosity would soon work in their favour.

Eventually, the Gauls found a way to get up on to the

Capitoline Hill, which they approached stealthily in the dead of night. By this stage, the watchmen and guard dogs were sleeping, but as soon as the first Gaul tried to climb over the fortress walls, Juno's geese raised the alarm. The noise woke Marcus Manlius, consul of the Roman Republic, who lifted the Gaul back over the walls and alerted his fellow Romans to the attack.

Bitter fighting ensued, and the Gauls soon realized there was no way they were going to conquer the heart of the Roman city, forcing them to retreat. Each year, the Romans held a procession to commemorate the event, led by, of course, a golden goose.

Pyramus and Thisbe

In another of Ovid's teleological poems in *Metamorphoses*, he uses a tragic love story to describe why the fruits of the mulberry bush are red. In distant Babylonia, a young boy called Pyramus lived next door to a girl named Thisbe. They were fond friends as children and that soon gave way to a deep love in their teens. But their families were far from amicable and both sides disallowed the union.

The two lovers were banned from seeing one another and would communicate only through a small crack in the wall between their homes. This continued for some time, until they decided to defy their parents and meet at night outside the city walls under a mulberry bush that bore white fruit.

Thisbe arrived first, wearing a veil to hide her face. But soon after she arrived she was all of a sudden confronted by a lioness that had come to drink from the stream. In fear, she ran away and hid in a cave, dropping her veil in her haste. The lioness grabbed at the veil with its bloody jaws and soon ambled on its way. When Pyramus arrived he noticed the paw prints in the dust and became anxious. Then he saw on the ground the bloodstained veil and was convinced that Thisbe had been mauled to death.

In his grief, Pyramus took out his sword and plunged it into his side, his blood splattering the white fruit of the tree with its purple-red hue. Thisbe then returned to see her lover dying beneath the tree. With a call to the gods to immortalize their unrequited love in the colour of the berries, and a plea for the two to be buried in one tomb, she fell on his sword and died at his side.

The keen-eyed Shakespeare fan will notice that this myth is the clear inspiration for his great tragedy

Romeo and Juliet, and the story of Pyramus and Thisbe is even played out in a deliberately ridiculous skit in *A Midsummer Night's Dream*.

Aeolus and the Winds

Among the many elements of nature that the Greeks and Romans personified as heroes and deities were the winds. Aeolus was the wind-keeper, and in *The Aeneid*, Juno offers him a nymph as a wife in exchange for his releasing favourable winds on to Aeneas' fleet to speed him closer to the founding of Rome.

The north wind was called Aquilo in Latin and Borealis in Greek (hence the term 'aurora borealis' for the Northern Lights), and was the violent and cold bringer of winter. He became quite smitten with the Athenian princess Oreithyia, and, in the manner of the times, enveloped her in a dense cloud and raped her, producing four children.

The east wind was Vulturnus (Latin) or Eurus (Greek), which was famed for bringing hot, humid storms. The south wind was Auster (Latin) or Notus (Greek), and it is from this personification that we get the name for Australia, and it is from the same root as 'Austria' and – confusingly – the word 'east'. (It is thought that Italy's land mass pointing in a south-easterly direction made it easy to perceive the rising sun of the east as coming from the south.)

The west wind was Favonius (Latin) or Zephyrus (Greek). As his Latin name describes, he is a favourable wind, heralding the blossoming of spring, flowers and fruit from the west. Both he and the god Apollo had fallen in love with a young Greek prince called Hyacinth. The two vied for the boy's affections, and Apollo was eventually chosen. Favonius saw the two playing discus together, and in an uncharacteristic ire he blew the discus back, which knocked the poor boy on the head and killed him. In his grief, Apollo created the hyacinth flower from the prince's blood.

CHAPTER 9:

NORSE
MYTHOLOGY

WHO WERE THE NORSE PEOPLE?

The Norsemen, or 'Northmen', originated from the northern European countries of Scandinavia during the Viking Age, from the eighth to the eleventh centuries. Known for their naval prowess, the Vikings, the explorers of the Norse world, set sail in their longships and invaded, pillaged and settled on the lands of Europe and western Russia.

Norse mythology, which flourished before the Christianization of Scandinavia, concerned the stories of the pagan gods, heroes and kings told in Scandinavia, northern Germany and Iceland. Although not committed to writing until the eleventh century – a process that continued until the eighteenth century – the stories themselves predated this time by hundreds of years,

Because of the Vikings' influence across Europe, and because existing records of Nordic mythology lasted until relatively recently, the usage of Nordic mythology and its iconography in the modern day may surprise you.

GODS AND GODDESSES

The Nordics possessed a complex and colourful polytheistic religion to rival the Greeks. Like their Greek counterparts, the Nordic gods were each responsible for an important aspect of life, and each god could be offered dedications and prayer in exchange for guidance in their particular field.

The Norse gods were divided into two clans: the Aesir, warrior deities of the sky who resided in Asgard, and the Vanir, who were linked to fertility and the earth and were based in Vanaheim. The universe over which they presided was split into nine worlds over three levels: the Asgard, the home of the Aesir, the Midgard 'Middle Earth', which was the home of humans, and the Niflheim, which was the home of the dead. Each of the nine worlds was connected by the World Tree, known as Yggdrasil, and each world was inhabited by a curious mix of humans, dwarves, elves, gods and other oddities. Asgard was the holiest of the nine worlds, and it could be reached via a rainbow bridge.

The Basis of the Norse Religion

Odin

As the father of the gods and the king of Aesir, it was Odin's duty to sit atop his throne in Asgard and (rather heroically for a god with just one eye) observe the goings on in each of the nine worlds, aided and abetted by his two ravens and two wolves, who acted as his protectors and messengers. Odin was the god of war, not to mention wisdom and poetry, and he also had strong links to the dead and the slain.

It also seems Odin was partial to alcohol, choosing to consume only wine. In fact, Odin's missing eye had been traded for a drink – although in that instance it had been for a cup full of water from the well of wisdom, from which Odin derived his immense knowledge, rather than for a large glass of Chardonnay. Regardless, Odin's one remaining eye did more than the work of two, burning as bright as the sun as he peered over the worlds. (Which is another interesting example of a myth created to help explain the movement of the sun in the sky.)

Odin's trademarks were his unfailing spear and his ring, from which another eight rings grew every ninth night. If he hadn't always been so intoxicated, Odin could probably have made himself a nice line in jewellery.

What's in a Name?

One of the most notable influences of Norse mythology is found in our names for the days of the week. Monday and Sunday were named after the moon and sun respectively, with Tuesday to Friday dedicated each to a different deity. The Nordics took the Roman names for these days and simply transposed their own corresponding god onto each day, which seems to have stuck in the Germanic languages, including English.

The table below shows where our everyday terms for every day have come from:

Day	Old Norse	Pronounced	Dedicated to
Monday	Mánadagr	mana-dagr	the moon
Tuesday	Týsdagr	tus-dagr	Tyr, god of justice
Wednesday	Óðinsdagr	othins-dagr	Odin, god of war, wisdom and poetry
Thursday	Þórsdagr	thors-dagr	Thor, god of protection and thunder
Friday	Frjádagr	frya-dagr	Freyja, goddess of love

Day	Old Norse	Pronounced	Dedicated to
Saturday	Laugardagr	laugar-dagr	Saturn, god of harvest
Sunday	Sunnudagr	sunu-dagr	the sun

Tyr

Son of Odin, Tyr was the god of war and his name derived from the same root as 'Zeus', 'Jupiter' and 'divine' – simply meaning 'god' across a range of Indo-European languages. Tyr was responsible for tying up the ferocious wolf monster, Fenrir, but at significant cost.

Fenrir had been brought to Asgard by Odin in order that he and his fellow gods could keep close watch over him. Alarmed at the animal's growth, Odin charged his son Tyr with feeding and taming the wild beast in the hope it might prevent him from destroying the Nine Worlds. Upon learning that his own fate was bound to Fenrir's, Odin decided the wolf must be tied up forever more. The gods duly attempted to tie him up with chains, but the great beast simply broke through them.

After a series of failed attempts, the gods enlisted the help of the elves, who crafted a special ribbon from the hair of a bearded lady which, they reassured Odin, would hold the wolf down. To help gain Fenrir's trust, Tyr bravely placed his right hand in the wolf's mouth but soon found it bitten clean off when Fenrir realized he was being bound by an unbreakable tie.

Thor

An enormous physical presence, Thor was the god of thunder and Odin's oldest son. He carried with him a colossal hammer with which he beat the crop (and his opponents), and the noise of which brought thunder. His enormous girdle doubled his strength and he wore a pair of iron gauntlets to help him control his hammer.

In a quest to determine whether physical power was more important than mental, Thor and Loki, a trickster and a descendent of the giants, travelled to the land of the giants to test their respective skills. Having acquired two companions en route, Thailfi and another, the four travellers finally arrived at their destination to be faced with derision – the giants thought it funny that Thor, whom they had heard so much about, was terribly tiny in size. Yet, despite their scepticism, the giants accepted a series of challenges from Thor and his companions.

The first contest saw Loki take on one giant in an eating contest. The table was piled high with meat, more than the giants had ever seen before. After gamely accepting the challenge, the two began to eat with the contest finally ending in a draw. However, it soon transpired that the giant had not only eaten the meat but all the bones too, which meant Loki had been defeated.

Next, their companion Thialfi challenged another giant to a race. But although Thialfi moved incredibly fast, his fellow competitor was even faster, able to reach the end of the race and turn back to meet Thialfi halfway again.

Thor then took on three challenges of his own. The first was a drinking contest, in which he attempted to consume mead from a gigantic horn in one go. Thor drank until he thought he would explode, and yet when he looked down he saw he had only managed to drain the horn by a small amount. Second, Thor was challenged to pick up a huge grey cat. Despite using all of his might he was only able to lift one paw of the massive beast. In his third and final task, Thor challenged the giants to a fight. In the light of Thor's recent failures, the giants conceded to allow him to fight Elli, an old scullery maid, rather than themselves. However, once again Thor was defeated.

But all was not what it seemed. Despite their initial derision, the giants confessed that they were in fact intimidated by Thor's enormous strength and, as such, had decided to employ a few tricks during the contest. In the eating contest Loki had been pitted against the giant that represents fire, which eats everything in its path. Thialfi's speed race had been against the giant that represents thought, which is always faster than action. And in the challenges undertaken by Thor, he had been able to show some great feats of might, despite the tactics employed by his giant adversaries. In his drinking challenge, the bottom end of the horn was in fact being filled with water from the entire ocean, and yet Thor was able to visibly lower it. The heavy cat was, in fact, the Midgard serpent, which wraps itself around the entire world, and yet Thor had been able to shift one of its paws. And, finally, the belligerent old maid had been Old Age herself, which no one can defeat, all of which seemed to suggest that mental strength will always triumph over physical prowess.

Freyja and Frigg

Primary goddess of Vanir, Freyja is the goddess of love, beauty and sexuality; the daughter of the sea god, Njord, and the giantess, Skadi; and the sister of Freyr, the god of fertility. Somewhat confusingly, according to other Germanic mythologies Freyja is also cognate with Frigg, her grandmother and the wife of Odin (see page 198). Such overlaps are too great to be ignored, and it is thought this division of one character into two distinct deities came quite late on.

As the goddess of fertility, Freyja had quite a sexual appetite and built herself something of a reputation, and she was also adept at practising the Norse magic *seidr*, which she employed to manipulate the desires, health and destiny of the gods.

Having one night dreamt of owning the shiniest and most glorious piece of gold, Freyja set out the following morning to track it down. Her journey, which, unbeknownst to her, was being observed by the mischievous Loki, took Freyja to the land of the dwarves. Once she had reached her destination, Freyja descended into the dwarves' cave, and became immediately entranced by the most brilliant and intricately crafted gold necklace she had ever seen. Despite Freyja offering several riches in exchange for the necklace, the four dwarves in attendance maintained they had no need for more silver or gold; the only way they would agree to hand over the necklace was if she spent a night with each of them.

Overcome with desire for the adornment, Freyja happily consented to their wishes. Having witnessed the whole affair, Loki returned to report the scene to Odin. A little displeased on hearing the news, Odin sent

Loki to retrieve the necklace from Freyja while she slept, which he managed by first transforming himself into a fly so he could enter her palace, and then into a flea so he could bite her face so she would turn to one side and he could undo the necklace clasp.

Freyja awoke to find the necklace gone and knew immediately Loki was to blame and that he would only have done so at the behest of Odin. She begged Odin for the necklace back, to which he finally consented, but only on one condition: Freyja was to set discord, hatred and unceasing war among the mortals in Midgard; and so we have greed and desire to blame for all disharmony in the world.

Freyr

One day, when Odin was otherwise engaged, Freyr took the opportunity to sit atop his godly throne. Taking in the magnificent view of all the nine worlds, Freyr's attention was drawn to Jotunheim, the land of the giants, and, specifically, a particularly beautiful young giantess called Gerdr. Freyr became obsessed with her beauty, and yet he could tell no one of his plight – he could not risk anyone finding out he had been sitting on Odin's throne.

Concerned for Freyr's wellbeing, his family sent the servant Skirnir to find out what was wrong with his master. Freyr explained his love for the giant Gerdr and convinced Skirnir to travel to Jotunheim to woo her on his behalf. He was given Freyr's automatic giant-fighting sword and a horse that was equipped to gallop through the ring of fire that encircled Gerdr's home.

Initially, Gerdr refused the offer, even when accompanied by a bribe of gifts, commenting that a giant could never love a Vanir god, as Freyr was. Unrelenting, Skirnir resorted to force, threatening the giantess with an eternity of hunger and unrequited desire, so she graciously accepted the proposal and wed Freyr.

The Norse Gods' Family Tree

Hel

Daughter of Loki and the giantess Angrboda, and the sister of Fenrir (the beastly wolf), Jormungand (the serpent wrapped around the world) and Sleipnir (Odin's eight-legged horse), Hel was the goddess of death, banished to the ghastly underworld by the other gods. Her ghastly appearance, with her skull fully exposed on one side of her face, meant she cut a terrifying figure.

As ruler of the underworld, Hel was responsible for judging the dead that came to her world (also known as Hel) and inflicting upon those that had sinned considerably in life eternal and brutal punishments. Her deadly torture chamber, from which were emitted loud screams, was made out of venomous snakes and sat atop an island of corpses in the middle of a river. Incredulously, some of the dead tried to escape from this awful chamber by means of a Naglfar – a boat made entirely out of the nail-clippings of the corpses.

To compound the awful surroundings, the entrance to Hel was guarded by a monstrous dog named Garmr. His face dripped with the blood of those souls who had tried in vain to escape their grim fate in the underworld.

Brynhildr

After Norse people died in battle, they would be taken either to Valhalla, Odin's palace of the slain, or to Freyja's Folkvangr hall. Odin's female warriors became his Valkyries and, in exchange for immortality, they had to decide which warriors would die and live in battle. Brynhildr was one of these immortals and it was her task to pick the loser of a battle between two kings.

Although she knew which king Odin wanted to be slain, Brynhildr decided to pick the other one, for which she was punished. Odin rescinded her immortality and set her on top of a huge mountain in the Alps, surrounded by an impenetrable ring of fire. Anyone who was able to reach her would receive her hand in marriage.

There are a few different versions of the myth, but one story involves a brave young chap called Siegfried (or Sigurd) who was the first to be able to break through the flames to reach Brynhildr. They fell in love on top of the mountain and he gave her a ring that produced reams of gold for the wearer. Before their nuptials, Siegfried visited King Gjuki and his wife, Grimhild. The queen wanted Siegfried to marry her own daughter, Gudrun, and administered a potion that made him forget all about Brynhildr. Siegfried and Gudrun were then married.

Aware that poor Brynhildr was alone on top of the mountain waiting for her fiancé to return, Grimhild sent her son Gunnar to marry Brynhildr in Siegfried's place. But Gunnar was incapable of penetrating the ring of fire, leaving the onus on Siegfried to make the leap in the guise of Gunnar. Fulfilling Odin's spell, Brynhildr married the man she thought was Gunnar and returned with him.

Siegfried's wife, Gudrun, revealed in a heated argument with Brynhildr that it was in fact Siegfried, and not Gunnar, who had rescued her. Enraged, Brynhildr incited the younger brother of Gunnar and Gudrun to kill Siegfried in his sleep. However, it was only on his death that Brynhildr realized she had loved Siegfried all along, and so she leapt upon his burning funeral pyre and the two were sent to Hel together.

The End: Ragnarök

Dotted throughout the tales of Norse mythology are references to a cataclysmic event that will see the end of most of the world. Known as Ragnarök ('end of rulers') and taking place at some point in the future, it will herald the end of Odin's reign, not to mention the demise of many other major gods. This terrifying apocalypse will come bearing a few tell-tale signs: three years of endless winter will kick-start proceedings and three cocks will crow – one waking the giants, another the gods, and the third raising the dead in Hel.

The sun and moon will be consumed and the stars will cease to shine, and humans will lose their morality and will be turned against one another. The ferocious wolf, Fenrir, will be released from his chains and the guard dog of Hel, Garmr, will howl at the entrance to the underworld.

The tree upon which the whole universe sits, Yggdrasil, will shake and groan, and Jormungand will writhe around, causing a great stir. Various beasts will kill various gods, and there will be huge battles in all worlds.

Eventually, fire will spread across everything and the

world will sink into the ocean – at which point the doom and gloom will cease and the world will be resurrected, fertile and fresh. Some of the gods will remain or will be reborn, and misery, greed and wickedness will have become extinct.

SELECTED BIBLIOGRAPHY

Books:

The Mythology Bible by Sarah Bartlett
(Godsfield Press, 2009)

Chinese Myths and Legends by Lianshan Chen
(Cambridge University Press, 2011)

*Mythology: The Complete Guide to Our Imagined
Worlds* by Christopher Dell (Thames and
Hudson, 2012)

The Library of Greek Mythology by Apollodorus, trans.
Robin Hard (Oxford Paperbacks, 2008)

The Oxford Companion to World Mythology by David
Leeming (Oxford University Press, 2009)

*The Greek and Roman Myths: A Guide to the Classical
Stories* by Philip Matyszak (Thames and Hudson, 2010)

Mesoamerican Mythology: A Guide to the Gods, Heroes, Rituals and Beliefs of Mexico and Central America by Kay Almere Read and Jason J. Gonzalez (OUP USA, 2002)

Websites:

Godchecker.com

Greekmythology.com

Maori.info

Pantheon.org

Wikipedia

INDEX

(page numbers in italic type refer to illustrations)